Dewdrops And Sunshine: A Collection Of Poems About Little Children

John Philip Newman

Dewdrops and Sunshine.

A COLLECTION OF POEMS ABOUT LITTLE CHILDREN.

EDITED BY

Mrs. J. P. NEWMAN,

And Dedicated to her Many Friends, Old and Young.

———— •♦• ————

NEW YORK:

NELSON & PHILLIPS.

CINCINNATI: HITCHCOCK & WALDEN.

1873.

AH! what would the world be
     to us
   If the children were no more?
We should dread the desert behind us
   Worse than the dark before.
They are better than all the ballads
   That ever were sung or said;
For they are living poems,
   And all the rest are dead.

Whittier.

Preface.

ITTLE children are the pure sun-
shine of earth. How beautifully these
tender rays dance and skip across
our life's pathway, making every
footprint glisten with the radiance of the
bright celestial. Alas! how many "Dew-
drops," like diamond settings in the sun-
shine, fall from silken eye-lashes, moistening
the green sods of the valley, and shutting out
for a brief moment of time the joyous sun-
shine of the loving mother's heart. I have
endeavored, in the selections that make up
this little volume, to gather some of the
bright sunshine of childhood, while the
dewdrops reflect in its clear rays all the
prismatic colors of the rainbow that spans
the bright hereafter.

I have been gathering the poems that are
sound in this and its companion volume,

" Mother, Home, and Heaven," for many years past, but the duties of a Pastor's wife have never, until now, allowed me time to arrange them.

I am indebted to my friends both North and South, who, when they learned I was arranging my collection in book-form, sent me many of their gleanings, which have materially aided in making up this volume.

Some of these poems are waifs gathered from newspapers and magazines, and it has been impossible to ascertain all the writers' names.

I claim little, if any, talent as a poet, but have been able to gain the *entree* into the sanctum sanctorum of the Muses, and have endeavored from their abundant store-house to bring out the new and the old.

If those who read find as much pleasure as I have found in selecting and arranging, I shall with joy exclaim, " The end crowns the work."   EVANGELINE.

DEWDROPS AND SUNSHINE.

My Lambs.

I LOVED them so,
   That when the Elder Shepherd
     of the fold
Came, covered with the storm, and
   pale and cold,
And begged for one of my sweet lambs
   to hold,
     I bade him go.

     He claimed the pet —
A little, fondling thing, that to my
   breast
Clung always, either in quiet or un-
   rest:
I thought of all my lambs I loved him best,
    And yet — and yet —

I laid him down
In those white, shrouded arms, with bitter
   tears;
For some voice told me that, in after-years,
He should know naught of passion, grief,
   or fears,
   As I had known.

And yet again
That Elder Shepherd came.   My heart grew
   faint.
He claimed another lamb! with sadder
   plaint,
Another!   She who, gentle as a saint,
   Ne'er gave me pain.

Aghast, I turned away!
There sat she, lovely as an angel's dream,
Her golden locks with sunlight all agleam,
Her holy eyes with heaven in their beam!
   I knelt to pray.

"Is it thy will?
My Father, say, must this pet lamb be given?
O! thou hast many such, dear Lord, in
   heaven."
And a soft voice said, "Nobly hast thou
   striven;
   But—peace, be still."

O, how I wept,
And clasped her to my bosom with a wild
And yearning love!   My lamb, my pleasant
    child!
Her, too, I gave.   The little angel smiled,
        And slept.

        "Go! go!" I cried.;
For once again that Shepherd laid his hand
Upon the noblest of our household band.
Like a pale specter, there he took his stand,
        Close to his side.

        And yet how wondrous sweet
The look with which he heard my passion-
    ate cry,
"Touch not my lamb! for him, O, let me
    die!"
"A little while," he said, with smile and
    sigh,
        "Again to meet."

        Hopeless I fell;
And when I rose, the light had burned so
    low,
So faint, I could not see my darling go:
He had not bidden me farewell; but O!
        I felt farewell

More deeply, far,
Than if my arms had compassed that slight
    frame;
Though could I but have heard him call
    my name,
"Dear mother!"——But in heaven 't will
    be the same;
      There burns my star!

      He will not take
Another lamb, I thought, for only one
Of the dear fold is spared to be my sun,
My guide, my mourner when this life is done;
      My heart would break.

      O, with what thrill
I heard Him enter! but I did not know
(For it was dark) that He had robbed me so.
The idol of my soul—he could not go—
      O heart! be still!

      Came morning.   Can I tell
How this poor frame its sorrowful tenant
    kept?
For waking tears were mine; I, sleeping,
    wept,
And days, months, years, that weary vigil
    kept.
      Alas!   "Farewell!"

How often it is said!
I sit and think — I wonder too, sometime —
How it will seem when, in that happier
    clime,
It never will ring out like funeral chime,
      Over the dead.

      No tears! no tears!
Will there a day come that I shall not weep?
For I bedew my pillow in my sleep.
Yes, yes; thank God, no grief that clime
    shall keep!
      No weary years!

      Ay, it is well;
Well with my lambs and with their earthly
    guide;
There, pleasant rivers wander they beside,
Or strike sweet harps upon its silver tide —
      Ay, it is well!

      Through the dreary day,
They often come from glorious light to me;
I cannot feel their touch, their faces see,
Yet my soul whispers, they do come to me:
      Heaven is not far away!

Little Mary's Wish.

H AVE seen the first robin of spring, mother
    dear,
  And have heard the brown darling sing:
You said, 'Hear it and wish, and 't will
    surely come true;'
  So I've wished such a beautiful thing!

"I thought I would like to ask something
    for *you ;*
  But I could n't think what there could be
That you'd want while you had all these
    beautiful things ;
  Besides, you have papa and me!

"So I wished for a ladder; so long that
    't would stand
  One end by our own cottage door,
And the other go up past the moon and the
    stars,
  And lean against heaven's white floor.

"Then I'd get you to put on my pretty
    white dress,
  With my sash and my darling new shoes;
Then I'd find some white roses to take up
    to God —
  The most beautiful ones I could choose —

"And you and dear papa would sit on the
    ground
  And kiss me, and tell me 'Good-by;'
Then I'd go up the ladder far out of your
    sight,
  Till I came to the door in the sky!

"I wonder if God keeps the door fastened
    tight?
  If but *one* little crack I could see,
I would whisper, 'Please, God, let this little
    girl in;
  She's as tired as she can be!

"'She came all alone from the earth to the
    sky;
  For she's always been wanting to see
The gardens of heaven, with their robins
    and flowers;
  Please, God, is there room there for me?'

"And then, when the angels had opened
   the door,
  God would say, 'Bring the little child
    here;'
But he'd speak it so softly I'd not be afraid;
  And he'd smile just like you, mother
    dear!

" He would put his kind arms round your
    dear little girl,
  And I 'd ask him to send down for you,
And papa, and cousin, and all that I love —
    O dear! don't you wish 't would come
    true ? " ·

The next spring-time, when the robins came
    home,
  They sang over grass and flowers
That grew where the foot of the ladder
    stood
  Whose top reached the heavenly bowers.

And the parents had dressed the pale, still
    child,
  For her flight to the summer land,
In a fair white robe, with one snow-white
    rose
  Folded tight in her pulseless hand.

And now at the foot of the ladder they sit,
  Looking upward with quiet tears,
Till the beckoning hand and the fluttering
    robe
  Of the child, at the top appears!
                  Mrs. L. M. Blinn.

The Child and the Flowers.

AST thou been in the woods with
the honey-bee?
Hast thou been with the lamb in the
pastures free?
With the hare through the copses and din-
gles wild?
With the butterfly on the heath, fair child?
Yes; the light fall of thy bounding feet
Hath not startled the wren from the mossy
seat;
Yet hast thou ranged the green forest-dells,
And brought back a treasure of buds and
bells.

Thou know'st not the sweetness of antique
song,
Breathed o'er the names of that flowery
throng;
The woodbine, the primrose, the violet dim,
The lily that gleams by the fountain's brim:
These are old words, that have made each
grove
A dreamy haunt for romance and love;
Each sunny bank, where faint odors lie
A pledge for the gushing of Poesy.

Thou know'st not the light wherewith fairy
    lore
Sprinkles the turf and the daisies o'er;
Enough for thee are the dews that sleep,
Like hidden gems, in the flower-urns deep;
Enough the rich crimson spots that dwell
'Midst the gold of the cowslip's perfumed
    cell;
And the scent by the blossoming sweet-brier
    shed,
And the beauty that bows the wood-hya-
    cinth's head.

O happy child, in thy fawn-like glee,
What is remembrance or thought to thee!
Fill thy bright locks with those gifts of
    spring,
O'er thy green pathway their colors fling;
Bind them in chaplet and wild festoon —
What if to droop and to perish soon!
Nature hath mines of such wealth, and thou
Never wilt prize its delights as now;

For a day is coming to quell the tone
That rings in thy laughter, thou joyous
    one!
And to dim thy brow with a touch of care
Under the gloss of its clustering hair;

And to tame the flash of thy cloudless eyes
Into the sadness of autumn skies;
And to teach thee that grief hath her need-
    ful part
'Midst the hidden things of each human
    heart!

Yet shall we mourn, gentle child, for this?
Life hath enough of yet holier bliss!
Such be thy portion: the bliss to look
With a reverent spirit through Nature's
    book;
By fount, by forest, by river's line,
To track the paths of a Love divine;
To read its deep meanings — to see and hear
God in earth's garden—and not to fear!

Little Feet.

N castle halls, or cottage homes,
Wherever guileless childhood roams,
O, there is nothing half so sweet
As busy tread of little feet!

The sighing breeze, the ocean's roar,
The purling rill, the organ's power,
All stir the soul; but none so deep
As tiny tread of little feet.

When we go forth, at early morn,
To meet the world and brave its scorn,
Adown the garden walk so neat
We see the prints of little feet.

At eve, when homeward we repair,
With aching limbs and brow of care,
And voices ring out clear and sweet —
Then comes the rush of little feet.

But when the angel Death has come,
And called the flow'rets from our home,
Oppressive silence reigns complete —
We miss the sound of little feet.

Then tools are safe, no dishes stray,
No doors go slamming all the day;
But O, 't would give us pleasure sweet
To hear again those noisy feet!

Soft night hath come; all are asleep;
Yes, all but me — I vigil keep;
Hush, hush, my heart, and cease to beat:
Was that the step of little feet?

Yes, mother, 't is the softened tread
Of him you miss and mourn as dead;
And often in your sweetest sleep
You'll dream of hearing little feet.

. And when this pilgrimage is o'er,
And you approach that blissful shore,
The first to run your soul to greet,
Will be your darling's little feet.

The Bright Side.

Our Idol.

CLOSE the door lightly, bridle the
 breath;
 Our little earth-angel is talking with
 Death.
Gently he woos her — she wishes to stay;
His arms are about her — he bears her away.

Music comes floating down from the dome;
Angels are chanting the sweet welcome home.
Come, stricken weeper, come to the bed!
Gaze on the sleeper — our idol is dead!

Smooth out the ringlets, close the blue eye;
No wonder such beauty was claimed in the
 sky!
Cross the hands gently o'er the white breast,
So like a bright spirit strayed from the blest;
Bear her out softly — this idol of ours —
Let her grave-slumbers be 'mid the sweet
 flowers.

2

Two Jewels.

TWO buds plucked from the tree,
  Two birdies flown the nest,
  Two little darlings snatched
    From a fond mother's breast.
Two little snow-white lambs
  Gone from the shelt'ring fold,
Two little narrow graves
  Down in the church-yard cold.

Two little drooping flowers
  Growing in purer air,
Blooming fragrant and bright
  In the Gardener's care.
Two little tender birds
  Flown far from fear and harm,
Two little snow-white lambs
  In the good Shepherd's arm.

Two little spirits more
  Singing with voices sweet,
Flinging their crowns of gold
  Down at their Saviour's feet.
Free from all earthly care,
  Pure from all earthly stain,
O, who would bring them back
  To this drear world again!

The Leak in the Dyke.

THE good dame looked from her cottage
  At the close of the pleasant day,
And cheerily called to her little son
  Outside the door at play:

"Come, Peter, come! I want you to go,
  While there is light to see,
To the hut of the blind old man who lives
  Across the dyke, for me;
And take these cakes I made for him—
  They are hot and smoking yet;
You have time enough to go and come
  Before the sun is set."

Then the good wife turned to her labor,
  Humming a simple song,
And thought of her husband, working hard
  At the sluices all day long;
And set the turf a-blazing,
  And brought the coarse black bread;
That he might find a fire at night,
  And find the table spread.

And Peter left the brother,
  With whom all day he had played,
And the sister who had watchèd their sports
  In the willow's tender shade;

And told them they'd see him back be-
  fore
  They saw a star in sight:
Though he wouldn't be afraid to go
  In the very darkest night,
For he was a brave, bright fellow,
  With eye and conscience clear;
He could do whatever a boy might do,
  And he had not learned to fear.
Why, he wouldn't have robbed a bird's
  nest,
  Nor brought a stork to harm,
Though never a law in Holland
  Had stood to stay his arm!

And now, with his face all glowing,
  And eyes as bright as the day
With the thoughts of his pleasant errand,
  He trudged along the way;
And soon his joyous prattle
  Made glad a lonesome place—
Alas! if only the blind old man
  Could have seen that happy face!
Yet he somehow caught the brightness
  Which his voice and presence lent;
And he felt the sunshine come and go
  As Peter came and went.

And now, as the day was sinking,
  And the winds began to rise,
The mother looked from her door again,
  Shading her anxious eyes;
And saw the shadows deepen,   .
  And birds to their homes come back,
But never a sign of Peter
  Along the level track.
But she said, "He will come at morn-
    ing,
  So I need not fret nor grieve —
Though it is n't like my boy at all
  To stay without my leave."

But where was the child delaying?
  On the homeward way was he,
And across the dyke while the sun was
    up
  An hour above the sea.
He was stopping now to gather flowers,
  Now listening to the sound,
As the angry waters dashed themselves
  Against their narrow bound.
"Ah! well for us," said Peter,
  "That the gates are good and strong,
And my father tends them carefully,
  Or they would not hold you long!

You 're a wicked sea," said Peter;
   " I know why you fret and chafe;
You would like to spoil our lands and
     homes,
   But our sluices keep you safe!"

But hark!   Through the noise of waters
   Comes a low, clear, trickling sound;
And the child's face pales with terror,
   And his blossoms drop to the ground.
He is up the bank in a moment,
   And, stealing through the sand,
He sees a stream not yet so large
   As his slender, childish hand.
'Tis a leak in the dyke!   He is but a boy,
   Unused to such fearful scenes;
But, young as he is, he has learned **to**
     know
   The dreadful thing that means.
A leak in the dyke!   The stoutest heart
   Grows faint that cry to hear,
And the bravest man in all the land
   Turns white with mortal fear.
For he knows the smallest leak may **grow**
   To **a** flood in a single night;
And he knows the strength of the **cruel**
     sea
   When loosed in its angry might.

And the boy!——He knows well the
    danger,
  And, shouting a wild alarm,
He forces back the weight of the sea
  With the strength of his single arm!
He listens for the joyful sound
  Of a footstep passing nigh;
And lays his ear to the ground to catch
  The answer to his cry.
And he hears the rough winds blowing,
  And the waters rise and fall,
But never an answer comes to him,
  Save the echo of his call.
He sees no hope, no succor;
  His feeble voice is lost;
Yet what shall he do but watch and
    wait,
  Though he perish at his post!

So, faintly calling and crying
  Till the sun is under the sea;
Crying and moaning till the stars
  Come out for company,
He thinks of his brother and sister,
  Asleep in their safe, warm bed;
He thinks of his father and mother,
  Of himself as dying—and dead:

And of how, when the night is over,
 They must come and find him at last;
But he never thinks he can leave the
  place
 Where duty holds him fast.

The good dame in the cottage
 Is up and astir with the light,
For the thought of her little Peter
 Has been with her all night.
And now she watches the pathway,
 As yestereve she had done;
But what does she see so strange and black
 Against the rising sun?
Her neighbors are bearing between them
 Something straight to her door;
Her child is coming home, but not
 As he ever came before!

"He is dead!" she cries; "my darling!"
 And the startled father hears,
And comes and looks the way she looks,
 And fears the thing she fears:
Till a glad shout from the bearers
 Thrills the stricken man and wife—
"Give thanks, for your son has saved our
  land,
 And God has saved his life!"

So, there in the morning sunshine
  They knelt about the boy;
And every head was bared and bent
  In tearful, reverent joy.

'T is many a year since then; but still,
  When the sea roars like a flood,
Their boys are taught what a boy can do
  Who is brave, and true, and good.
For every man in that country
  Takes his son by the hand,
And tells him of little Peter,
  Whose courage saved the land.
They have many a valiant hero,
  Remembered through the years,
But never one whose name so oft
  Is told with loving tears.
And his deed shall be sung by the cradle,
  And told to the child on the knee,
So long as the dykes of Holland
  Divide the land from the sea!

Phebe Carey.

PROMISE of youth! fair as the form
  Of Heaven's benign and golden bow,
Thy shining arch begirds the storm,
  And sheds a light on every woe.

J. G. Brooks.

A Christmas Carol for the Children.

 LITTLE wee infant is sleeping,
The angels bright vigils are keeping,
The stars from yon heaven are peep-
    ing,
And singing in anthems of joy :
The wise men are led to the manger,
They gather around the fair stranger;
The great and the good of the nation
Come to offer their hearts' adoration,
At his feet to present their oblation ;
    Men and angels worship the Boy.

How strange, that just one little mortal,
Who here hath just entered earth's portal,
Of mother so meek and so lowly —
Why is it the great and the holy,
    Enraptured, there gather around?
O'er his face what a halo is beaming!
All around them a glory is gleaming!
Of all this, canst thou tell us the meaning?
    Why the heavens with music resound?

Why the heralding angels are flying,
And heavenly trumpets, all vieing?
Who is this bright beautiful stranger —
This little one born in the manger?

From whence doth the "Wonderful"
   spring?
'T is the "Star of the East" hath arisen,
"The Light" which Jehovah hath given;
'T is the Saviour, the meek and the lowly,
The Son of the Father most holy,
   Our Prince and our heavenly King!

Let the nations of earth all adore him,
And cast their sweet incense before him;
   Each heart in its gratitude sing!
Rejoice that our Father in heaven
His Son, as Redeemer, hath given;
   O'er the earth let the glad tidings ring!
                  Eva Alice.

Wait and See.

WHEN' my boy, with eager ques-
   tions,
   Asking how, and where, and when,
   Taxes all my store of wisdom,
     Asking o'er and o'er again
Questions oft to which the answers
   Give to others still the key,
I say, to teach him patience,
   "Wait, my little boy, and see."

And the words I taught my darling
  Taught to me a lesson sweet:
Once when all the world seemed darkened
  And the storm about me beat,
In the "children's room" I heard him,
  With a child's sweet mimicry,
To his baby brother's questions
  Saying wisely, "Wait and see."

Like an angel's tender chiding
  Came the darling's words to me;
Though my Father's ways were hidden,
  Bidding me still wait and see.
What are we but restless children,
  Ever asking what shall be?
And the Father, in his wisdom,
  Gently bids us "wait and see."

Open the Door.

OPEN the door for the children,
    Tenderly gather them in;
  In from the highways and hedges,
    In from the places of sin.
Some are so young and so helpless!
  Some are so hungry and cold!
Open the door for the children,
  Gather them into the fold.

Open the door for the children;
  See! they are coming in throngs;
Bid them sit down to the banquet,
  Teach them your beautiful songs!
Pray you the Father to bless them,
  Pray you that grace may be given;
Open the door for the children:
  "Of such is the kingdom of heaven."

Open the door for the children;
  Take the dear lambs by the hand;
Point them to truth and to goodness;
  Send them to Canaan's fair land.
Some are so young and so helpless!
  Some are so hungry and cold!
Open the door for the children,
  Gather them into the fold.

"Now I Lay Me Down to Sleep."

N the quiet nursery chambers,
  Snowy pillows yet unpressed,
  See the forms of little children
  Kneeling, white-robed for their rest;
All in quiet nursery chambers,
  While the dusky shadows creep,
Hear the voices of the children—
  "Now I lay me down to sleep."

On the meadow and the mountain
　Calmly shine the winter stars,
But across the glistening lowlands
　Slant the moonlight's silver bars;
In the silence and the darkness,
　Darkness growing still more deep,
· Listen to the little children
　Praying God their souls to keep.

"If we die"—so pray the children
　And the mother's head droops low,—
(One from out her fold is sleeping
　Deep beneath the winter's snow,)
"Take our souls,"—and past the casement
　Flits a gleam of crystal light,
Like the trailing of his garments,
　Walking evermore in white.

To my Wee Bairn.

CREEP awa', my bairnie,
　Creep before ye gang;
Listen with both ears
　To your old granny's sang.
If ye gang as far as I,
　The road ye 'll think na lang,
Creep awa', my bairnie,
　Creep before ye gang.

Creep awa', my bairnie,
  Ye 're ower young to learn
To tot up and down yet,
  My bonnie, bonnie bairn;
Better creeping, carefu',
  Than falling wi' a bang,
Hurting a' your wee brow —
  Creep before ye gang.

The little birdie fa's
  When it tries ower soon to fly;
Folk are sure to tumble
  When they climb ower high.
Those who do not walk aright
  Are sure to come to wrang;
Creep awa', my bairnie —
  Creep before ye gang.
                          Willie Winkie.

Little Chatterbox.

THEY call me "Little Chatterbox;"
  My name is little May.
I have to talk so much, because
  I have so much to say.

And, O, I have so many friends!
  So many; and, you see,
I can't help loving them, because
  They, every one, love me.

I love my papa and mamma;
I love my sisters, too;
And if you 're very, very good,
I guess that I'll love you!

'But I love God the best of all;
He keeps me all the night;
And when the morning comes again,
He wakes me with the light.

I think it is so nice to live!
And yet, if I should die,
The Lord would send his angels down
And take me to the sky.

How Little Katie Knocked at the Door of Heaven.

LITTLE heads all brown and golden,
Little forms on bench and stool,
Drooped so languid, warm, and
weary,
In the hill-side village school;
For the sun was fiercely beaming
Through the windows, wide and bare;
Myriad flies were going, coming,
Droning, in the heated air.

Katie's ringlets fell the lowest;
  Softly closed each fringéd lid;
And the sweet cheeks' deepening flushes
  'Neath the golden vail were hid.
Sleeping, dreaming, now is Katie,
  Of that lovely morn in May,
When her little brother Charlie
  With an angel went away;

Floating through the gates of glory,
  Trembling, fluttering to His breast,
Which the precious olden story
  Tells us is our lasting rest.
Now she dreams that back he's flying
  To her little, lonely heart;
Now she clasps him! sighing, crying,
  Sobbing, with her joy's great smart.

Sobbing—woke. With arms caressing,
  Little Bella, soft and low,
Whispered, "What's the matter, Katie?
  Tell me why you're crying so."
But the teacher, school dismissing,
  Said, "Dear children, haste away!
See the clouds, so dark and lowering!
  It will rain ere close of day."

3

Sadly, slowly, from the doorway—
  While the rest did hasten quick—
Came the child; and once more Bella
  Said, "Poor Katie! are you sick?"
"O, dear Bella, 't is that only
  I have dreamed, that grieves me so!
I *must* see my brother Charlie!
  To my brother I must go!

"Mother says he went to heaven:
  But, though we may go to him,
Back to us he 's never coming;"
  And her sweet blue eyes grew dim.
"Then go right to *him*," cried Bella.
  "Ah! I do not know the way.
In a dreadful box they put him
  While in bed, so ill, I lay."

"Are you *sure* he went to heaven?"
  "Yes, I *know* it, Bella, dear."
"Then," said Bella, smiling brightly,
  "Katie, *I* can take you there:
I saw where they put your brother.
  Katie, come; this very even,
Hand in hand we'll go together—
  Hand in hand we'll go to heaven."

Forth they set upon their journey,
  Heedless of the gathering gloom;
Little pilgrims, true and earnest,
  Sure that Charlie would make room.
Only once did Bella murmur,
  "*Can* you enter? Are you *sure?*"
Flushed with coming joy, she answered,
  "He would *run* to ope the door."

"Do you think he's very happy?"
  "*Very!*" was the eager cry.
"Has he playthings up in heaven?
  Can they get them there, so high?'
"'T is with angels now he's playing;
  Angels with such lovely wings!
With the gold and purple rainbows,
  Stars, and other heavenly things."

"O!" cried Bella, interrupting,
  Looking up, in great dismay:
"See! 't is raining fast and faster;
  Now we cannot go to-day."
"But we 've almost got to heaven;
  Turning back would be a sin.
Charlie's *waiting* for his sister—
  We can hurry and run in."

Bella, peering through the darkness,
    Said, " O, yes, I see the door ! "
" Where ? O, where ? " cried Katie, breath-
        less.
        " There ! "   And pointing straight be-
            fore,
Katie saw the village church-yard
    Rising through the misty gloom ;
Near, a black and iron door-way,
    Leading to a vaulted tomb.

Then with bitter disappointment,
    Swelling higher, wave on wave,
Out she sobbed, " *O, is that heaven ?*
    'T is a great and lonely grave ! "
" But 't is here they took your brother ;
    Katie, 't is the very place ;
And you said he'd gone to heaven ! "—
    Then a smile came in her face.

" Let us go and knock, dear Katie.
    When to enter we have tried,
We shall find it bright and lovely ;
    Heaven is on the *other* side."
Fast and faster fell the rain-drops
    From the sky with clouds o'erspread,
And the floor of heaven resounded
    To the thunder's mighty tread.

Still the little children, clasping
  Hand in hand, and pale with fear,
Hastened onward to the entrance —
  Guardian angels watching near.
Now they 're there ! The golden moment
  Of the dreamer, Kate, has come,
And the child — her sweet lips pressing
  On the door of Charlie's home —

Knocked, with all her strength and power.
  Mournful Echo only heard :
Little brother never heeding,
  Never answering a word.
Then a piteous cry, imploring,
  From her grieved heart's inmost core,
Came : " O, Charlie, 't is your sister !
  Charlie, wont you ope the door ? "

" May be, Katie, he *can't* hear you
  Through the thunder and the rain ;
Wait a little while," urged Bella,
  " Then, dear Katie, knock again."
Strong in faith, the loving sister
  Once, and once again, did try :
" Charlie ! Charlie ! " only Echo
  Answered back the yearning cry.

" Do you hear him ?   Is he coming ? "
   Bella asked, with wistful tone.
" Once I thought I heard his little
   Shoes come pattering — but they 're
      gone ! "
" May be, Katie, he is playing
   With the angels, far away,
In a lovely flower garden,
   Where the sunshine stays all day."

" O," sobbed Katie, " *wont* he hear me ?
· *Wont* he come, with joy, to see
His own sister ?   Does he love those
   Little angels more than me ? "
" Knock once more, just once," urged
   Bella.
Then the soft and tiny hand,
With faint faith, for entrance pleaded
   'Midst that shining angel band.

" Charlie ! dear, sweet, darling Charlie !
   Please to come !   O, come and see !
'T is your sister — don't love angels,
   Little brother, more than me ! "
With her eyes all wild with longing,
   Closer to the door she moved,
Listening, listening, listening, listening,
   For the step so dearly loved.

On the ground, all wet and streaming,
  Down she threw herself at last,
With a cry, "O Charlie! Charlie!"—
  Then a silence. Hope is past.
Pale, and frightened at her anguish,
  Bella said, with loving sigh,
"We'll go home now, and to-morrow
  Let us come again and try."

Shuddering, she rose, but tearless.
  "I shall come here nevermore;
Never ask for brother Charlie
  At this dark and dreary door."
Back, with little feet and dresses
  Wet and dripping, slow they went:
Little hearts with grief so heavy,
  Little heads with sorrow bent.

At the door stood Katie's mother,
  Filled with undefined alarms;
When the child, with bitter crying,
  Sprang into her loving arms.
"Mother," sobbed she—tears now stream-
    ing
  Piteously adown her face—
"I *so* wanted brother Charlie!
  Bella took me to the place—

"To the very door of heaven —
  Then, above the thunder's din,
Loud I knocked, and said, 'O Charlie!
  Little brother! let me in!'"
Then her eyes grew dark with anguish.
  "Mother, how can I begin
Telling you the cruel story? —
  Charlie would not let me in!"*

Darling, grieving little Katie,
  All too young to understand,
'T was the *spirit* of her brother
  Floated to that heavenly land!
Here his mortal body resteth
  In the earth — returned to earth;
While the angels there are singing
  Welcome to his soul's new birth.

It may be, that ere the violets
  Through the earth again have risen,
God may call thee, little Katie —
  God may point the way to heaven.
Knock thou then, O little pilgrim!
  Charlie will, with eager wing,
Fly to ope the blessed portal,
  While the heavenly choir shall sing,

* The identical words of the child.

"Glory! Glory! Halleluia!
Let the joyful anthems ring!
Jesus loves the little children;
  To his feet your Katie bring."
While on earth his precious blessing
  To these little ones was given;
"Suffer them to come unto me;
  Chide them not; of such is heaven."
                              Aunt Fanny.

Weighing the Baby.

OW many pounds does the baby
    weigh?
  Baby who came but a month ago;
How many pounds from the growing
    curl
  To the rosy joint of the restless toe?

Grandfather ties the kerchief knot,
  Tenderly guides the swinging weight,
And carefully over his glasses peers
  To read the record —" Only eight."

Softly the echo goes around;
  The father laughs at the tiny girl;
The fair young mother sings the words,
  While grandmother smooths the golden
    curl;

And stooping above the precious thing,
  Nestles a kiss within a prayer;
Murmuring softly, " Little one,
  Grandfather did not weigh you fair."

Nobody weighed the baby's smile,
  Or the love that came with the helpless
    one;
Nobody weighed the threads of care
  From which the woman's life is spun.

No index tells the mighty worth
  Of a little baby's quiet breath;
A soft, unceasing metronome,
  Patient and faithful unto death.

Nobody weighed the baby's soul,
  For here on earth no weight there be
That could avail.   God only knows
  Its value in eternity.

Only eight pounds to hold a soul
  That seeks no angel's silver wing,
But shrines it in this human guise
  Within so fair and small a thing.

O, mother, laugh your merry note!
  Be gay and glad; but don't forget
From baby's eyes look out a soul
  That claims a home in Eden yet.

Baby Fingers.

EN fat little fingers, so taper and
neat!
Ten fat little fingers, so rosy and
sweet!
Eagerly reaching for all that comes near,
Now poking your eyes out, now pulling your
hair;
Smoothing and patting with velvet-like
touch,
Then digging your cheek with a mischievous
clutch;
Gently waving good-bye with infantine
grace,
Then dragging your bonnet down over your
face;
Beating pat-a-cake, pat-a-cake, slow and
sedate,
Then tearing a book at a furious rate;
Gravely holding them out, like a king, to
þe kissed,
Then thumping the window with tightly-
closed fist;
Now lying asleep, all dimpled and warm,
On the white cradle-pillow, secure from all
harm.

O, dear baby hands! how much love you
    unfold
In the weak, careless clasp of those fingers'
    soft hold!
Keep spotless, as now, through the world's
    evil ways,
And bless with fond care our last weariful
    days.

———————

Polly.

BROWN eyes,   Catching flies
  Little nose;   On the pane;
Dirt pies,   Deep sighs—
  Rumpled clothes. Cause not plain;

Torn books,   Bribing you
  Spoiled toys;   With kisses
Arch looks,   For a few
  Unlike a boy's;   Farthing blisses;

Little rages,   Wide awake,
  Obvious arts;   As you hear,
(Three her age is,) " Mercy's sake,
  Cakes, tarts; .   Quiet, dear! "

Falling down   New shoes,
  Off chairs;   New frock;
Breaking crown Vague views
  Down stairs;   Of what's o'clock;

When it's time   Thinks it odd,
  To go to bed,   Smiles away;
And scorn sublime Yet may God
  For what is said;   Hear her pray!

Folded hands,   Bedgown white,
  Saying prayers,   Kiss Dolly;
Understands   Good night!—
  Not, nor cares;   That's Polly,

      Fast asleep,
        As you see;
      Heaven keep
        My girl for me!

Little Will.

A GREAT crowd of people had gathered around
  A small ragged urchin stretched out on the ground
In the midst of the street; and some cried, "For shame!"
And others, "Can any one tell us his name?"
For that poor little body, now bleeding and still,
Was all that was left of once bright little Will.

A great heavy cart had come rattling that way
Where Willie and others were busy at play,
And the poor little fellow, now stretched on
    the stones,
Seemed only a mass of bruised flesh and
    crushed bones.
But still there was life! and a kind doctor
    said,
"We must take the child home and put him
    to bed.
He must have all the care we can possibly
    give,
And it may be the poor little fellow will
    live."

But, alas for poor Willie! he *had* no nice
    home;
He lived in an alley, in one little room;
And his poor mother, working from earliest
    light,
Had often no supper to give him at night.

But joy for poor Willie! for not far away
From the place where, all bleeding and shat-
    tered, he lay,
Is a very large house standing back from
    the street,
With every thing round it so quiet and neat,

Which many good people had built in His
    name
Who healed all the sick when from heaven
    He came;
And who promises blessings that ever endure
To those who shall comfort the sick and
    the poor.
So there, in a room large, and cheerful, and
    bright,
Little Willie was laid on a pillow so white.
The walls with bright pictures were covered
    all o'er;
Will never had seen such a clean place before.
Long rows of small beds, with small tables
    between,
The coverlids white, and the beds painted
    green;
And so many children, all sick, but so bright,
Will almost forgot his great pain at the sight.

But the poor little boy suffered terrible pain
When the good surgeon came to examine
    again
Those poor little limbs; and he said that
    next day
He must bring his sharp knives and cut both
    legs away.

O! how could he bear it? O! what should
    he do?
So small and alone, he could never get
    through.
And then he knew well that he never could
    run
And play with the boys, as before he had
    done.
Poor Willie! he felt that in all that great city
There was no one to help him and no one
    to pity.

It was night: in the hospital ward all was
    still,
Save the low moans of anguish from poor
    little Will,
When a dear little girl in the very next bed
Turned round on her pillow and lovingly
    said,
"Little boy, what's the matter? are you
    very ill?"
"O yes," said poor Willie; "and what is
    worse still,
The doctor is going to hurt my legs so
To-morrow; I never can bear it, I know."
"But Jesus will help you," said dear little Sue;
"He suffered and died, you know, Willie,
    for you."

The child was astonished, and thus made
    reply:
"Why, Susie, who's Jesus? and what made
    him die?"
"O, Willie, how sad! I thought every one
    knew.
You don't go to Sunday-school; isn't that
    true?"
"No, I never have been," the boy made reply;
"But tell me of Jesus, and what made him
    die."

"Well, Jesus," said Susie, "came down long
    ago,
Because he was sorry we all suffered so,
And would be so naughty. And he was a
    child,
Just as little as we, but so gentle and mild;
And when he grew up he went all through
    the land,
And healed all the sick with a touch of his
    hand;
And he took little children right up on his
    knee—
O, Willie, I wish it had been you and me!
But soon cruel men caught Jesus one day,
And beat him, and mocked him, and took
    him away,

4

And nailed him with nails to a great cross
    of wood.
O! wasn't it hard, when he'd done them
    such good?
How he must have loved us, to die on the
    tree!"
"But," said Will, "if he's dead, how can he
    help *me*?"
"Why, I'll tell you," said Susie; "though
    now he's in heaven,
In the Book he has left us a promise is given,
That whenever we want him he'll come to
    our aid.
I'm so sure he loves me I'm never afraid;
I know that he comes to this hospital here,
And though folks can't *see* him, they *feel* he
    is near.
I know, for I've tried it again and again:
He helps us bear sickness, and sorrow, and
    pain."

"O how good!" said the boy, with a long,
    thankful sigh:
"But I am so small that he might pass me
    by;
So I'll put up my hand, just so he can see,
Then he'll know that I want him, and come
    right to me."

When the bright sun peeped in on that little
    white bed
The hand was still raised, but dear Willie
    was dead !
The sad look of pain had gone from his face,
And the sweetest of smiles had taken its
    place ;
For far off in heaven, that beautiful land,
Kind Jesus had seen little Will's lifted hand ;
The smile on his face Jesus' kissing had
    given,
And he waked in the morning with Jesus
    in heaven.

Dear friends who have read this sweet story,
    you see
That trusting in Jesus will save you and me.
O that all who of Jesus' great mercy have
    heard,
Would, like dear little Willie, *take Him at*
    his word!   *M. L. V. W.*

Youth.

GATHER the rosebuds while you may ;
    Old Time is still a-flying ;
And the same flower that blooms to-day
    To-morrow shall be dying.
                Herrick.

The Little Angels.

HERE 'S many an empty cradle,
　There 's many a vacant bed;
There 's many a lonesome bosom,
　Whose joy and light has fled.

For thick in every grave-yard
　The little hillocks lie;
And every hillock represents
　An angel in the sky.

The Fisher's Child.

THROUGH all the morn the fishers
　　toiled
　With wonderful success;
Yet naught but curses passed the lips
　That had such cause to bless.

Three hardy men were in the boat,
　While, leaning o'er its side,
A little child with dimpled hand
　Was plashing in the tide.

Anon his arm grew motionless,
　His large wild eyes were bent
Upon the darkling depths below,
　As on a book intent;

And soothing lessons, strangely sweet,
  From out the lake he read,
While fleecy trains of summer clouds
  Were floating overhead.

Too heavenly pure his visions grew
  For waking hours below,
Then sleep upon his dreamy eyes
  Let fall the lids of snow.

Long hours he sweetly slumbered on,
  Till tumult met his ear;
He woke, and found the hardy men
  Were agonized with fear.

Black, ragged clouds across the sky
  In masses wild were whirled,
The bearers of a mighty wind
  That seemed to shake the world.

The lake appeared an angry sea,
  And with each boiling wave
Still nearer to the rocky shore
  The tiny vessel drave.

In fixed despair the fishers sat
  Amid the dashing spray,
And each upon the other looked,
  And wished he dared to pray.

Then spoke the child, "We need not fear,
  Our Lord must with us be,
For all the morn his loving face
  Was bending down to me."

He ceased, then knelt, and to the clouds
  Upraised his trustful eye:
Although they could not hear his prayer,
  They saw his God's reply.

In safety round the rugged point
  At once the boat was swept,
To where, within a sheltered bay,
  The quiet waters slept.

From peril saved, full oft had they
  Returned to sin again;
But now beside the child they stood
  Forever altered men.

The Little Shoe.

FOUND it here — a worn-out shoe,
  All mildewed with time and wet with
      dew;
'T is a little thing;—many pass it by,
With never a thought, or word, or sigh;
Yet it stirs in my spirit a hidden well,
And in eloquent tones, of the past doth tell.

It tells of a little fairy form
That bound my heart with a magic charm;
Of bright blue eyes, and golden hair,
That ever shed joy and sunlight there;
Of a prattling voice so sweet and clear,
And of tiny feet that were ever near.

It tells of hopes that with her had birth,
Deep buried now in the silent earth;
Of a heart that had met an answering tone,
Which again is left alone — alone;
Of days of watching and anxious prayer;
Of a night of sorrow and dark despair.

It tells of a form that is cold and still;
Of a little mound upon yonder hill
That is dearer far to a mother's heart
Than the classic statues of Grecian art.
Ah! strangers may pass with a careless air,
Nor dream of the hopes that are buried there.

O ye who have never o'er loved ones wept —
Whose brightest hopes have ne'er been swept
Like a pure white cloud from the morning
  sky,
Like the wreath of mist from the mountain
  high;
Like the rainbow, beaming a moment here,
Then melting away to its native sphere;

Like rose leaves loosed by the zephyr's
   sigh;
Like that zephyr wafting its perfume by;
Like the wave that kisses some grateful spot,
Then passes away, yet is ne'er forgot;
If your life-hopes like these have never fled,
Then ye cannot know of the tears I shed.

Ye cannot know what a little thing
From memory's silent fount can bring
The voice and form that were once so dear.
Yet there are hearts, were they only here,
That could feel with me, when, all wet with
   dew,
I found it this morning—this little shoe.
                 Mary E. Nealy

Our Little Queen.

OULD you have seen the violets
   That blossomed in her eyes;
Could you have kissed that golden
   hair,
   And drank those holy sighs;
You would have been her tiring-maid
   As joyfully as I,
Content to dress your little queen,
   And let the world go by.

Could you have seen those violets
  Hide in their graves of snow;
Drawn all that gold along your hand
  While she lay smiling so;
O, you would tread this weary earth
  As heavily as I;
Content to clasp her little grave,
  And let the world go by.

Pappy-Go-Lucky.

ERE you are, Flora and Lily. Ah,
    well!
  May as well settle what story to tell.
  This: of a darling, with cheeks
    rosy red;
Sunny hair, coiling in rings on his head;
Eyes always dancing with roguish delight —
Always—except when the lids droop at night.
" Happy-go-Lucky " we called him one day,
Half but in earnest and half but in play.
" S'ant call me names," quoth our mischiev-
  ous sprite.
" I'll tell my Pappy-Do-Lucky to-night."

" Pappy-Go-Lucky! " dear Grandmamma
  cried,
Both hands uplifted and eyes opened wide,

Cheeks all aflame, like the bloom on a peach,
"When did I *ever* hear just such a speech?"
"Well, he *is* lucky," rejoined the gay elf:
"Did n't he tell me so, all his own self?
Has n't you of'en heard my mamma say
Yare 's no luck in ye house when my papa 's
    away?
I 'se heard her say it, and sing it all fru,
Tause it 's a song tune; but yen it 's *yeal*
   true."

Grandmamma folded her knitting away,
Smoothed out the folds of her gown, soft
    and gray,
Took the wee laddie, then, up on her knee,
Holding his hands in hers, slowly said she:
"When *I* was young, little boys who would
   say
Such disrespectful words, even in play,
Had to be punished.   And so I think you,
My little grandson, should be punished too.
Therefore, when all the commandments
   you 've said,
I shall undress you and put you to bed."

"Whe-e-ew!" said our baby.   "*Yat's* aw-
   ful!   You bet!
Dramma, she finks ye wus *punshimunts* yet!

'All ye commanjums!' My doodness! I
'clare
I don' know *none* of 'em, 'cep' ye Lord's
Prayer.
Better pick out somefin' yat I *can* do.
Dess I knows *Muzzer Goose,* mose ye way
fru.
Try me on *yat,* and yen put me to bed.
My! but I'se dettin suts pains in my head!
When you has tucked in ye bedclo'es and
fings,
Wont I have jolly times, *jouncing ye springs!*"

Grandmamma bit her lips, frowned, and
looked vexed;
Sorely this infant her spirit perplexed.
"What *shall* I do?" she said, low, to herself:
"Surely, the rod I must take from the shelf."
Little pink ears caught the words, whispered
low;
Blue eyes danced merrily; all in a glow
Flushed the soft cheeks of this mischievous
sprite :
"Mus'n't back out!" he cried. "*Yat* isn't
right.
Dood drammas s'ouldn't tell *tawlys,*" he
said,
Roguishly shaking the curls on his head.

Grandma coughed queerly, winked fast, and
    then smiled.
How could she help it? "O, what a spoiled
    child!"
Said she at last, gravely shaking her head.
Then she undressed him, and put him to
    bed;
Lay down beside him, and spoiled all his
    fun
Of jouncing the springs. Pray, was not *that*
    well done?

When the dear papa came home to his tea,
Up to the nursery quickly sped he.
"Where is my curly head?" Then he
    espied
Grandma and boy, fast asleep, side by
    side.
"Something's gone wrong"—so the dear
    papa guessed—
"Else this gay youngster would not be un-
    dressed."
Wide the blue eyes opened, up popped the
    head:
"*Dramma and me, wese dot bofe sent to bed.*
Awful bad luck we has when you aint
    home,
Pappy-Do-Lucky, I'se dlad you has tome.

Dess I'll det up now an' do down to tea,
Don't wake up dramma," (sly rogue,) whis-
    pered he.
Thus ends my story, sweet Lily and Floy,
Of Pappy-Go-Lucky, and grandma, and
    boy.   *Mary E. C. Wyeth.*

────────◆────────

The Little People.

 DREARY place would be this earth
        Were there no little people in it;
    The song of life would lose its mirth
        Were there no children to begin it;

No little forms, like buds, to grow,
    And make th' admiring heart surrender;
No little hands on breast and brow,
    To keep the thrilling love-chords tender.

The sterner souls would grow more stern,
    Unfeeling nature more inhuman,
And man to stoic coldness turn,
    And woman would be less than woman.

Life's song, indeed, would lose its charm
    Were there no babies to begin it;
A doleful place this world would be
    Were there no little people in it.
                          J. G. Whittier.

"I Might Sometime Forget It."

THE chill November day was done,
    The working world home faring;
The wind came roaring through the
        streets,
        And set the gaslights flaring;
And hopelessly and aimlessly
    The scared old leaves were flying,
When, mingled with the soughing wind,
    I heard a small voice crying.

And, shivering on the corner, stood
    A child of four, or over;
No cloak or hat her small, soft arms
    And wind-blown curls to cover;
Her dimpled face was stained with tears;
    Her round, blue eyes ran over;
She cherished in her wee, cold hand
    A bunch of faded clover.

And, one hand round her treasure, while
    She slipped in mine the other,
Half-scared, half-confidential, said,
    "O! please, I want my mother."
"Tell me your street and number, pet;
    Don't cry; I 'll take you to it."
Sobbing, she answered, "I forget:
    The organ made me do it.

"He came and played at Miller's step—
  The monkey took the money;
I followed down the street, because
  That monkey was so funny.
I 've walked about a hundred hours
  From one street to another;
The monkey 's gone; I 've spoiled my flowers;
  O! please, I want my mother."

"But what 's your mother's name? and
    what
  The street? Now think a minute."
"My mother's name is Mother Dear;
  The street — I can't begin it."
"But what is strange about the house?
  Or new — not like the others?"
"I guess you mean my trundle-bed —
  Mine and my little brother's.

"O dear! I ought to be at home
  To help him say his prayers;
He 's such a baby he forgets,
  And we are both such players;
And there 's a bar between to keep
  From pitching on each other,
For Harry rolls when he 's asleep.
  O dear! I want my mother."

The sky grew stormy; people passed
   All muffled, homeward faring.
"You 'll have to spend the night with me,"
   I said at last, despairing.
I tied a kerchief round her neck:
   "What ribbon 's this, my blossom?"
"Why don't you know!" she, smiling, said,
   And drew it from her bosom.

A card with number, street, and name!
   My eyes astonished met it;
"For," said the little one, "you see
   I might some time forget it;
And so I wear a little thing
   That tells you all about it;
For mother says she's very sure
   I should get lost without it."
                   Eliza Sproat Turner.

O WHAT a treasure of sweet thought
   Is here! what hope, and joy, and love,
All in one tender bosom brought,
   For the all-gracious Dove
To brood o'er silently, and form for heaven
Each passionate wish and dream to dear
   affection given   *Keble.*

Grace and Her Friends.

"YOUR walk is lonely, blue-eyed Grace,
　　Down the long forest road to school,
　Where shadows troop, in many a
　　　place,
　　From sullen chasm to sunless pool.
Are you not often, little maid,
Beneath the sighing trees afraid?"

"Afraid,—beneath the tall, strong trees
　　That bend their arms to shelter me,
And whisper down, with dew and breeze,
　　Sweet sounds that float on lovingly,
Till every gorge and cavern seems
Thrilled through and through with fairy
　　dreams?

"Afraid,—beside the water dim
　　That holds the baby-lilies white
Upon its bosom, where a hymn
　　Ripples forth softly to the light
That now and then comes gliding in,
A lily's budding smile to win?

"Fast to the slippery precipice
　　I see the nodding harebell cling;
In that blue eye no tear there is;
　　Its hold is firm—the frail, free thing!

5

The harebell's Guardian cares for me,
So I am in safe company.

"The woodbine clambers up the cliff
    And seems to murmur, 'Little Grace,
The sunshine were less welcome if
    It brought not every day your face.'
Red leaves slip down from maples high,
And touch my cheek as they flit by.

"I feel at home with every thing
    That has its dwelling in the wood;
With flowers that laugh, and birds that
        sing, —
    Companions beautiful and good,
Brothers and sisters every-where;
And over all, our Father's care.

"In rose-time or in berry-time, —
    When ripe seeds fall, or buds peep out, —
When green the turf, or white the rime,
    There 's something to be glad about.
It makes my heart bound just to pass
The sunbeams dancing on the grass.

"And where the bare rocks shut me in
    Where not a blade of grass will grow,
My happy fancies soon begin
    To warble music, rich and low,

And paint what eyes could never see :
My thoughts are company for me.

"What does it mean to be alone ?
  And how is any one afraid
Who feels the dear God on his throne
  Beaming like sunshine through the shade,
Warming the damp sod into bloom,
And smiling off the thicket's gloom ?

"At morning, down the wood-path cool
  The fluttering leaves make cheerful talk ;
After the stifled day at school,
  I hear, along my homeward walk,
The airy wisdom of the wood,
Far easiest to be understood.

"I whisper to the winds ; I kiss
  The rough old oak, and clasp his bark ;
No farewell of the thrush I miss ;
  I lift the soft vail of the dark,
And say to bird, and breeze, and tree,
'Good-night ! Good friends you are to
      me !'"   *Lucy Larcom.*

———————

A SWEET new blossom of humanity,
Fresh fallen from God's own home to flower
      on earth.   *Gerald Massey.*

Annie and Willie's Prayer.

'WAS the eve before Christmas:
"Good-night," had been said,
And Annie and Willie had crept
into bed.
There were tears on their pillows, and tears
in their eyes,
And each little bosom was heaving with
sighs;
For to-night their stern father's command
had been given
That they should retire precisely at seven —
Instead of at eight — for they troubled him
more
With questions unheard of than ever before.
He had told them he thought this delusion
a sin,
No such creature as "Santa Claus" ever
had been;
And he hoped, after this, he should never
more hear
How he scrambled down chimneys with
presents each year.
And this was the reason that two little
heads
So restlessly tossed on their soft, downy
beds.

Eight, nine, and the clock on the steeple
    tolled ten :
Not a word had been spoken by either, till
    then,
When Willie's sad face from the blanket did
    peep, .
And whispered, " Dear Annie, is 'ou fast
    aseep ? "
"Why no, Brother Willie," a sweet voice
    replies,
" I 've long tried in vain, but I can't shut
    my eyes ;
For somehow it makes me so sorry because
Dear papa has said there is no ' Santa Claus.'
Now *we* know there is, and it can't be denied,
For he came every year before mamma died.
But, then, I 've been thinking that she used
    to pray,
And God would hear every thing mamma
    would say,
And may be she asked him to send Santa
    Claus here
With the sack full of presents he brought
    every year."
"Well, why tan't we pay dust as mamma
    did den,
And ask Dod to send him with pesents
    aden ? "

"I 've been thinking so, too,"—and with-
   out a word more
Four little bare feet bounded out on the
   floor,
And four little knees the soft carpet pressed,
And two tiny hands were clasped close to
   each breast.

"Now, Willie, you know we must firmly
   believe
That the presents we ask for we 're sure to
   receive;
You must wait just as still till I say the
   'Amen,'
And by that you will know that your turn
   has come then."

"Dear Jesus, look down on my brother and
   me,
And grant us the favor we 're asking of
   thee.
I want a wax dolly, a tea-set, and ring,
And an ebony work-box that shuts with a
   spring:
Bless papa, dear Jesus, and cause him to see
That Santa Claus loves us as much as does
   he:
Don't let him get fretful and angry again
At dear Brother Willie and Annie. Amen."

"Pease, Desus, 'et Santa Taus tum down
 to-night,
And bing us some pesents before it is
 'ight;
I want he sood div' me a nice 'ittle sed,
With bight shinin' 'unners, and all painted
 'ed;
A box full of tandy, a book, and a toy,
Amen. And den, Desus, I 'll be a dood
 boy."

Their prayers being ended, they raised up
 their heads,
And, with hearts light and cheerful, again
 sought their beds.
They were soon lost in slumber, both peace-
 ful and deep,
And with fairies in dreamland were roaming
 in sleep.

Eight, nine, and the little French clock had
 struck ten,
Ere the father had thought of his children
 again :
He seems now to hear Annie's half-sup-
 pressed sighs,
And to see the big tears stand in Willie's
 blue eyes.

"I was harsh with my darlings," he men-
    tally said,
"And should not have sent them so early
    to bed:
But then I was troubled; my feelings found
    vent,
For bank stock to-day has gone down ten
    per cent.
But of course they've forgotten their troubles
    ere this,
And that I denied them the thrice-asked-for
    kiss;
But, just to make sure, I'll steal up to their
    door —
For I never spoke harsh to my darlings
    before."

So saying, he softly ascended the stairs,
And arrived at the door to hear both of
    their prayers;
His Annie's "Bless papa" drew forth the
    big tears,
And Willie's grave promise fell sweet on his
    ears.
"Strange — strange — I'd forgotten," said
    he, with a sigh,
How I longed when a child to have Christ-
    mas draw nigh."

" I 'll atone for my harshness," he inwardly
   said,
" By answering their prayers ere I sleep in
   my bed."
Then he turned to the stairs and softly went
   down,
Threw off velvet slippers and silk dressing-
   gown,
Donned hat, coat, and boots, and was out
   in the street —
A millionaire facing the cold, driving sleet !
Nor stopped he until he had bought every
   thing,
From the box full of candy to the tiny gold
   ring :
Indeed, he kept adding so much to his store
That the various presents outnumbered a
   score.
Then homeward he turned, when his holi-
   day load,
With Aunt Mary's help, in the nursery was
   stowed.
Miss Dolly was seated beneath a pine-tree,
By the side of a table spread out for her tea ;
A work-box, well filled, in the center was
   laid,
And on it the ring for which Annie had
   prayed :

A soldier, in uniform, stood by a sled
"With bright shining runners, and all paint-
    ed red."
There were balls, dogs, and horses; books
    pleasing to see;
And birds of all colors were perched in the
    tree;
While Santa Claus, laughing, stood up in
    the top,
As if getting ready more presents to drop.
Now as the fond father the picture surveyed,
He thought for his trouble he'd amply
    been paid,
And he said to himself, as he brushed off a
    tear,
"I'm happier to-night than I've been for a
    year;
I've enjoyed more true pleasure than ever
    before;
What care I if bank-stock falls ten per cent.
    more!
Hereafter I'll make it a rule, I believe,
To have Santa Claus visit us each Christ-
    mas Eve."
So thinking, he gently extinguished the
    light,
And, tripping down stairs, retired for the
    night.

As soon as the beams of the bright morning
    sun
Put the darkness to flight, and the stars one
    by one,
Four little blue eyes out of sleep opened wide,
And at the same moment the presents espied;
Then out of their beds they sprang with a
    bound,
And the very gifts prayed for were all of
    them found.
They laughed and they cried, in their inno-
    cent glee,
And shouted for papa to come quick, and see
What presents Old Santa Claus brought in
    the night,
(Just the things that they wanted!) and left
    before light.
"And now," added Annie, in voice soft and
    low,
"You'll believe there's a 'Santa Claus,'
    papa, I know;"
While dear little Willie climbed up on his
    knee,
Determined no secret between them should
    be,
And told, in soft whispers, how Annie had said
That their dear, blessed mamma, so long
    ago dead,

Used to kneel down and pray by the side
    of her chair,
And that God up in heaven had answered
    her prayer.
"Den we dot up, and payed dust well as
    we tood,
And Dod answered our payers; now, was n't
    he dood?"
"I should say that he was, if he sent you all
    these,
And knew just what presents my children
    would please.
(Well, well, let him think so, the dear little
    elf,
'T would be cruel to tell him I did it myself.")

Blind father! who caused your stern heart
    to relent,
And the hasty words spoken so soon to re-
    pent?
'T was the Being who bade you steal softly
    up stairs,
And made you his agent to answer *their*
    prayers.   *Mrs. Sophia P. Snow.*

THE paths that lead us to God's throne
Are worn by children's feet.

The Child's World.

GREAT, wide, beautiful, wonderful
world,
With the wonderful water round you
curled,
And the wonderful grass upon your breast —
Beautiful world, you are wondrously drest!

The wonderful sky is over me,
And the wonderful wind is shaking the tree;
It walks on the water, and whirls the mills,
And talks to itself on the tops of the hills.

You friendly earth! how far do you go
With the wheat-fields that nod, and the
rivers that flow;
With cities, and gardens, and cliffs, and isles,
And people upon you — for thousands of
miles?

Ah! you are so great, and I am so small,
I tremble to think of you, World, at all;
And yet when I said my prayers to-day,
A whisper inside me seeméd to say —

"You are more than the Earth, though you
are such a dot;
You can love and think, and the Earth
cannot!"

The Unfinished Prayer.

OW I lay me — say it, darling; "
  " Lay me," lisped the tiny lips
Of my daughter, kneeling, bending
  O'er her folded finger-tips.

" Down to sleep" — "To sleep," she mur-
    mured,
  And the curly head dropped low;
" I pray the Lord," I gently added,
  " You can say it all, I know."

" Pray the Lord" — the words came faint-
    ly —
  Fainter still — " My soul to keep; "
Then the tired head fairly nodded,
  And the child was fast asleep.

But the dewy eyes half opened
  When I clasped her to my breast,
And the dear voice softly whispered,
  " Mamma, God knows all the rest."

O, the trusting, sweet confiding
  Of the child-heart!   Would that I
Thus might trust my heavenly Father,
  He who hears my feeblest cry!

Bed-Time.

ROSEBUD lay in her trundle-bed,
   With her small hands folded above
     her head,
   And fixed her innocent eyes on me,
While a thoughtful shadow come over their
   glee.
"Mamma," she said, "when I go to sleep
I pray to the Father my soul to keep;
And he comes and carries it far away,
To the beautiful home where his angels stay.
I gather red roses and lilies so white,
I sing with the angels through all the long
   night;
And when, in the morning, I wake from my
   sleep,
He gives back the soul that I gave him to
   keep,
And I only remember, like beautiful dreams,
The garlands of lilies, the wonderful
   streams."

————————

A BABE in a house is a well-spring of pleas-
   ure; a messenger of peace and love;
A resting-place of innocence on earth; a link
   between angels and men. *Tupper.*

The God of My Childhood.

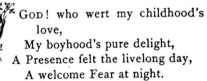

God! who wert my childhood's
    love,
    My boyhood's pure delight,
A Presence felt the livelong day,
    A welcome Fear at night.

They bade me call thee Father, Lord!
    Sweet was the freedom deemed;
And yet more like a mother's ways
    Thy quiet mercies seemed.

I could not sleep unless Thy hand
    Were underneath my head,
That I might kiss it if I lay
    Wakeful upon my bed.

And quite alone I never felt;
    I knew that Thou wert near —
A Silence tingling in the room;
    A strangely pleasant Fear.

I know not what I thought of Thee;
    What picture I had made
Of that Eternal Majesty
    To whom my childhood prayed.

I know I used to lie awake
  And tremble at the shape
Of my own thoughts, yet did not wish
  Thy terrors to escape.

With age Thou grewest more divine,
  More glorious than before;
I feared Thee with a deeper fear,
  Because I loved Thee more.

Thou broadenest out with every year
  Each breath of life to meet;
I scarce can think Thou art the same,
  Thou art so much more sweet.

FATHER, what hast Thou grown to now?
  A Joy all joys above;
Something more sacred than a Fear,
  More tender than a Love.

With gentle swiftness lead me on,
  Dear God, to see thy face;
And, meanwhile, in my narrow heart,
  O make thyself more space!
                              Faber.

THE good die first,
And they whose hearts are dry as summer's
    dust
Burn to the socket.   *Wordsworth.*

6

My Little Cousins.

LAUGH on, fair cousins, for to you
    All life is joyous yet;
    Your hearts have all things to pursue,
      And nothing to regret;
And every flower to you is fair,
    And every month is May;
You 've not been introduced to Care, —
    Laugh on, laugh on, to-day!

Old Time will fling his clouds ere long
    Before those sunny eyes;
The voice whose every word is song
    Will set itself to sighs;
Your quiet slumbers — hopes and fears
    Will chase their rest away;
To-morrow you 'll be shedding tears, —
    Laugh on, laugh on, to-day!

O yes, if any truth is found
    In the dull schoolman's theme, —
If friendship is an empty sound,
    And love an idle dream, —
If Mirth, youth's playmate, feels fatigue
    Too soon on life's long way,
At least he 'll run with you a league, —
    Laugh on, laugh on, to-day!

Perhaps your eyes may grow more bright
   As childhood's hues depart;
You may be lovelier to the sight,
   And dearer to the heart;
You may be sinless still, and see
   This earth still green and gay;
But what you are you will not be;
   Laugh on, laugh on, to-day!

O'er me have many winters crept
   With less of grief than joy;
But I have learned, and toiled, and wept—
   I am no more a boy!
I've never had the gout, 't is true,
   My hair is hardly gray;
But now I cannot laugh like you;
   Laugh on, laugh on, to-day!

I used to have as glad a face,
   As shadowless a brow;
I once could run as blithe a race
   As you are running now:
But never mind how I behave;
   Don't interrupt your play;
And though I look so very grave,
   Laugh on, laugh on, to-day!
                 Praed.

Baptism of a Child.

HE stood up in the meekness of a
          heart
Resting on God, and held her fair
          young child
Before her bosom, with its gentle eyes
Folded in sleep, as if its soul had gone
To whisper the baptismal vow in heaven.
The prayer went up devoutly with her faith
That it would be, even as he had prayed,
And the sweet child be gathered to the fold
Of Jesus.   As the holy words went on
Her lips moved silently, and tears, fast tears,
Stole from beneath her lashes, and upon
The forehead of the beautiful child lay soft
With the baptismal water.   Then I thought,
That to the eye of God, that mother's
          tears
Would be a deeper covenant — which sin
And the temptations of the world and death
Would leave unbroken — and that she would
          know,
In the clear light of heaven, how very strong
The prayer which pressed them from her
          heart had been,
In leading its young spirit up to God.
                                    N. P. Willis.

Maidenhood.

MAIDEN! with the meek brown
        eyes,
    In whose orbs a shadow lies
    Like the dusk in evening skies!
Standing with reluctant feet
Where the brook and river meet!
Womanhood and childhood fleet!
Gazing with a timid glance
On the brooklet's quick advance,
On the river's broad expanse!
O thou child of many prayers!
Life hath quicksands, life hath snares!
Care and age come unawares!
Bear a lily in thy hand;
Gates of brass cannot withstand
One touch of that magic wand.
Bear through sorrow, wrong, and ruth,
In thy heart the dew of youth,
On thy lips the smile of truth.

                        Longfellow.

GOD keep thee, child, with thy angel brow,
Ever as sinless and bright as now;
Fresh as the roses of earliest spring,
The fair, pure buds it is thine to bring.

Would that the bloom of thy soul could be,
Beautiful spirit! caught from thee!
Would that thy gift could anew impart
The roses that bloom for the pure in heart!
                              Lucy Hooper.

In School-Days.

STILL sits the school-house by the
        road,
    A ragged beggar, sunning;
Around it still the sumachs grow,
    And blackberry vines are running.

Within, the master's desk is seen,
    Deep scarred by raps official;
The warping floor, the battered seats,
    The jack-knife's carved initial;

The charcoal frescoes on its wall;
    Its door-step still betraying
The feet that, creeping slow to school,
    Went storming out to playing!

Long years ago a winter sun
    Shone over it at setting;
Lit up its western window-panes,
    And low eaves' icy fretting.

It touched the tangled golden curls,
   And brown eyes full of grieving,
Of one who still her steps delayed
   When all the school were leaving.

For near her stood the little boy
   Her childish favor singled;
His cap pulled low upon a face
   Where pride and shame were mingled.

Pushing with restless feet the snow
   To right and left, he lingered; —
As restlessly her tiny hands
   The blue-checked apron fingered.

He saw her lift her eyes; he felt
   The soft hand's light caressing;
And heard the tremble of her voice,
   As if a fault confessing.

'I'm sorry that I spelled the word:
   I hate to go above you,
Because,"— the brown eyes lower fell, —
   "Because, you see, I love you!"

Still memory to a gray-haired man
   That sweet child-face is showing;
Dear girl! the grasses on her grave
   Have forty years been growing!

He lives to learn, in life's hard school,
   How few who pass above him
Lament their triumph and his loss,
   Like her, — because they love him.
                J. G. Whittier.

Making a Little Grave.

OOM, gentle flowers! my child
      would pass to heaven!
    Ye looked not for her yet with
      your soft eyes,
O watchful ushers at death's narrow door!
But lo! while you delay to let her forth,
Angels, beyond, stay for her! One long kiss
From lips all pale with agony, and tears,
Wrung after anguish had dried up with fire
The eyes that wept them, were the cup of
    life
Held as a welcome to her. Weep, O
    mother!
But not that from this cup of bitterness
A cherub of the sky was turned away.
                N. P. Willis.

HEAVEN lies about us in our infancy.
                Wordsworth.

A Rocking Hymn.

SWEET baby, sleep: what ails my
    dear?
    What ails my darling, thus to cry?
    Be still, my child, and lend thy ear
    To hear me sing thy lullaby.
My pretty lamb, forbear to weep;
Be still, my dear; sweet baby, sleep.

Whilst thus thy lullaby I sing,
    For thee great blessings ripening be;
Thine eldest Brother is a King,
    And has a kingdom bought for thee.
Sweet baby, then, forbear to weep;
Be still, my babe; sweet baby, sleep.

A little infant once was He,
    And strength in weakness then was laid
Upon his virgin mother's knee,
    That power to thee might be conveyed.
Sweet baby, then, forbear to weep;
Be still, my babe; sweet baby, sleep.

Within a manger lodged thy Lord,
    Where oxen lay, and asses fed;
Warm rooms we do to thee afford,
    An easy cradle or a bed.
Sweet baby, then, forbear to weep;
Be still, my babe; sweet baby, sleep.

Thou hast, yet more to perfect this,
  A promise and an earnest got,
Of gaining everlasting bliss,
  Though thou, my babe, perceiv'st it not.
Sweet baby, then, forbear to weep;
Be still, my babe; sweet baby, sleep.

George Withers.

Baby's Shoes.

THOSE little, those little blue shoes!
Those shoes that no little feet use.
  O, the price were high
  That those shoes would buy,
Those little, blue, unused shoes!

For they hold the small shape of feet
That no more their mother's eyes meet;
  That, by God's good will,
  Years since stood still,
And ceased from their totter so sweet.

And O! since that baby slept,
So hushed, how the mother has kept,
  With a tearful pleasure,
  That little dear treasure,
And over them thought and wept!

For they mind her for evermore
Of a patter along the floor;
  And blue eyes she sees
  Look up from her knees
With the look that in life they wore.

As they lie before her there,
There babbles from chair to chair
  A little sweet face
  That's a gleam in the place,
With its little gold curls of hair.

Then O wonder not that her heart
From all else would rather part
  Than those tiny blue shoes
  That no little feet use,
And whose sight makes such fond tears
  start!

Little Birdie.

HAT does little birdie say,
    In her nest at break of day?
    "Let me fly," says little birdie,
    "Mother, let me fly away."
"Birdie, rest a little longer,
Till the little wings are stronger."
So she rests a little longer,
    Then she flies away.

What does little baby say,
In her bed at peep of day?
Baby says, like little birdie,
  " Let me rise and fly away."
" Baby, sleep a little longer,
Till the little limbs are stronger."
If she sleeps a little longer
  Baby, too, shall fly away.

Tennyson.

My Good-for-Nothing.

WHAT are you good for, my brave
      little man?
    Answer that question for me, if
      you can.
You, with your fingers as white as a nun, —
You, with your ringlets as bright as the sun:
All the day long, with your busy contriving,
Into all mischief and fun you are driving;
See if your wise little noddle can tell
What you are good for.   Now ponder it well."

Over the carpet the dear little feet
Came with a patter to climb on my seat;
Two merry eyes, full of frolic and glee,
Under their lashes looked up unto me;

Two little hands pressing soft on my face,
Drew me down close in a loving embrace;
Two rosy lips gave the answer so true:
"Good to love you, mamma, good to love
    you."   *Emily Huntington Miller.*

———————

CHILDHOOD, to thee I turn from life's alarms,
Serenest season of perpetual calms;
Turn with delight, and bid the passions cease,
And joy to think with thee I tasted peace.

———————

There's No Such Girl as Mine!

THERE'S no such girl as mine
    In all the wide world round;
    With her hair of golden twine,
    And her voice of silver sound.
Her eyes are as black as the sloes,
    And quick is her ear, so fine;
And her breath is as sweet as the rose,—
    There's no such girl as mine!

Her spirit so sweetly flows,
    Unconscious winner of hearts;
There's a smile wherever she goes,
    There's a sigh whenever she parts.

A blessing she wins from the poor,
  To court her the rich all incline;
She's welcome at every door, —
  O there's no such girl as mine!

She's light to the banquet hall,
  The balm to the couch of care;
In sorrow — in mirth — in all —
  She takes her own sweet share.
Enchanting the many abroad,
  At home doth she brightest shine;
'T were endless her worth to laud, —
  There's no such girl as mine!
                    Samuel Lover.

Baby's Feet.

TWO little feet, so small that both
      may nestle
    In one caressing hand;
  Two tender feet upon the untried
      border
    Of Life's mysterious land.

Dimpled, and soft, and pink as peach-tree
      blossoms
    In April's fragrant days —
How can they walk among the briery tangles
    Edging the world's rough ways?

These white-rose feet along the doubtful
    future
  Must bear a woman's load,
Alas! since woman has the heaviest burden,
  And walks the hardest road.

Love, for awhile, will make the path before
    them
  All dainty, smooth, and fair —
Will cull away the brambles, letting only
  The roses blossom there.

But when the mother's watchful eyes are
    shrouded
  Away from sight of men,
And these dear feet are left without her
    guiding,
  Who shall direct them then?

How will they be allured, betrayed, deluded,
  Poor little untaught feet! —
Into what dreary mazes will they wander?
  What dangers will they meet?

Will they go stumbling blindly in the dark-
    ness
  Of Sorrow's tearful shades?
Or find the upland slopes of Peace and
    Beauty,
  Whose sunlight never fades?

Will they go toiling up Ambition's summit,
    The common world above?
Or in some nameless vale, securely sheltered,
    Walk side by side in Love?

Some feet there be which walk Life's track
        unwounded,
    Which find but pleasant ways;
Some hearts there be to which this life is only
    A round of happy days.

But they are few.   Far more there are who
        wander
    Without a hope or friend:
Who find their journey full of pains and
        losses,
    And long to reach the end.

How shall it be with her, the tender stranger,
    Fair-faced and gentle-eyed,
Before whose unstained feet the world's rude
        highway
    Stretches so strange and wide?

Ah! who may read the future?   For our
        darling
    We crave all blessings sweet;
And pray that He who feeds the crying ravens
    Will guide the baby's feet.
                            Florence Percy.

How the Gates Came Ajar.

T WAS whispered one morning in
heaven
How the little child-angel, May,
In the shade of the great white portal
Sat sorrowing, night and day.
How she said to the stately warden —
He of the key and bar —
" O angel, sweet angel! I pray you
Set the beautiful gates ajar!
Only a little, I pray you,
Set the beautiful gates ajar!

" I can hear my mother weeping;
She is lonely; she cannot see
A glimmer of light in the darkness
When the gates shut after me.
O, turn me the key, sweet angel,
The splendors will shine so far!"
But the warden answered: " I dare not
Set the beautiful gates ajar!"
Spoke low, and answered: " I dare not
Set the beautiful gates ajar!"

Then rose up Mary the blesséd,
Sweet Mary, Mother of Christ;
Her hand on the head of the angel
She laid, and her touch sufficed;

7

Turned was the key in the portal;
  Fell ringing the golden bar;
And lo! in the little child's fingers
  Stood the beautiful gates ajar!
In the little child-angel's fingers
  Stood the beautiful gates ajar!

" And this key for future using
  To my blesséd Son shall be given:"
Said Mary, Mother of Jesus,
  Tenderest heart in heaven.
Now never a sad-eyed mother
  But may catch the glory afar,
Since safe in the Lord Christ's bosom
  Are the keys of the gates ajar;
Close hid in the dear Christ's bosom, —
  And the gates forever ajar!

An Italian Poem.

The Charmed Bird.

MOTHER, O mother! this morning,
    when Will,
  And Mary, and I, had gone out on
    the hill,
We stopped in the orchard to climb in the
  trees,
And break off the blossoms that sweetened
  the breeze;

Then right down before us, and close where
    we were,
There fluttered, and fluttered, a bird in the
    air.

"Its crest was so glossy, so bright were its
    eyes,
And its wings — O, their color was just like
    the skies!
And still as it chirped, and kept eddying
    round
In narrower circles, and nearer the ground,
We looked, and all hid in the leaves of the
    brake,
We saw, don't you think, O, the ugliest
    snake!"

Caressingly folding the child in her arms,
With thoughts of sweet birds in a world full
    of charms,
"My child," said the mother, "in life's later
    hours
Remember the morning you stopped for the
    flowers;
And still, when you think of the bird in the
    air,
Forget not, my love, that the serpent was
    there."   *Alice Carey.*

We are Seven.

A SIMPLE child,
    That lightly draws its breath,
And feels its life in every limb,
    What should it know of death?

I met a little cottage girl;
    She was seven years old she said;
Her hair was thick with many a curl
    That clustered round her head.

She had a rustic, woodland air,
    And she was wildly clad;
Her eyes were fair, and very fair; —
    Her beauty made me glad.

" Sisters and brothers, little maid,
    How many may you be ? "
    " How many !   Seven in all," she said,
    And wondering looked at me.

" And where are they ? I pray you tell."
    She answered, " Seven are we;
And two of us at Conway dwell,
    And two are gone to sea.

" Two of us in the church-yard lie,
    My sister and my brother;
And in the church-yard cottage I
    Dwell near them with my mother."

"You say that two at Conway dwell,
 And two are gone to sea,
Yet ye are seven! I pray you tell,
 Sweet maid, how this may be?"

Then did the little maid reply,
 "Seven boys and girls are we;
Two of us in the church-yard lie,
 Beneath the church-yard tree."

"You run about, my little maid;
 Your limbs they are alive;
If two are in the church-yard laid,
 Then ye are only five."

"Their graves are green, they may be seen,"
 The little maid replied,
"Twelve steps or more from my mother's
  door,
 And they are side by side.

"My stockings there I often knit,
 My kerchief there I hem;
And there upon the ground I sit,
 And sing a song to them.

"And often after sunset, sir,
 When it is light and fair,
I take my little porringer,
 And eat my supper there.

" The first that died was sister Jane;
  In bed she moaning lay,
Till God released her from her pain, —
  And then she went away.

" So in the church-yard she was laid;
  And when the grass was dry,
Together round her grave we played,
  My brother John and I. .

"And when the ground was white with
      snow,
  And I could run and slide,
My brother John was forced to go,
  And he lies by her side."

" How many are you, then," said I,
  " If they two are in heaven?"
Quick was the little maid's reply,
  " O, master, we are seven!"

"But they are dead; those two **are**
      dead;
  Their spirits are in heaven!"
'T was throwing words away; for still
The little maid would have her will,
  And said, "Nay, we are seven!"
                    Wordsworth.

To a Child.

CHILD! O new-born denizen
Of life's great city! on thy head
The glory of the morn is shed
Like a celestial benison!
Here at the portal thou dost stand,
And with thy little hand
Thou openest the mysterious gate
Into the future's undiscovered land.
By what astrology of fear or hope
Dare I to cast thy horoscope?
Like the new moon thy life appears;
A little stripe of silver light,
And widening outward into night
The shadowy disk of future years;
A prophecy and intimation,
A pale and feeble adumbration,
Of the great world of light that lies
Behind all human destinies.

Longfellow.

O, THEY are Thine,
These jewels of my life, not mine, not mine!
So keep them that the blossoms of their youth
Shall, in a gracious growth of love and truth,
With an abundant harvest honor thee.

Mrs. Butler.

The Little Frock.

COMMON light blue muslin frock
Is hanging on the wall,
But no one in the household now
Can wear a dress so small.

The sleeves are both turned inside out,
And tell of summer wear;
They seem to wait the owner's hands
Which last year hung them there.

'T was at the children's festival
Her Sunday dress was soiled—
You need not turn it from the light;
To me it is not spoiled!

A sad, and yet a pleasant, thought
Is to the spirit told
By this dear, little, rumpled thing,
With dust in every fold.

Why should men weep that to their home
An angel's love is given?
Or that before them she is gone
To blessedness in heaven?

Catharine Luders.

The Promise.

OD hath said, "Forever blesséd
Those who seek me in their youth;
They shall find the path of wisdom,
And the narrow way of truth."
Then, when evening shades shall gather,
We may turn our tearless eye
To the dwelling of our Father,
To our home beyond the sky,
Gently passing
To the happy land on high.

The Boy and His Angel.

MOTHER, I've been with an angel
to-day!
I was out all alone in the forest, at
play,
Chasing after the butterflies, watching the
bees,
And hearing the woodpecker tapping the
trees;
So I played, and I played, till, so weary I
grew,
I sat down to rest in the shade of a yew,

While the birds sang so sweetly high up on
    its top,
I held my breath, mother, for fear they
    would stop.

Thus a long while I sat, looking up to the
    sky,
And watching the clouds that went hurry-
    ing by,
When I heard a voice calling, just over my
    head,
That sounded as if 'Come, O brother!' it
    said;
And there, right over the top of the tree,
O mother, an angel was beck'ning to me!

"And, 'Brother,' once more, 'Come, O
    brother!' he cried,
And flew on light pinions close down by my
    side;
And, mother, O never was being so bright
As the one which then beamed on my won-
    dering sight!
His face was as fair as the delicate shell;
His hair down his shoulders in fair ringlets
    fell;
While his eyes, resting on me so melting
    with love,
Were as soft and as mild as the eyes of a dove;

And somehow, dear mother, I felt not
    afraid,
As his hand on my brow he caressingly
    laid,
And murmured, so softly and gently, to me,
'Come, brother, the angels are waiting for
    thee!'

"And then on my forehead he tenderly
    pressed
Such kisses—O, mother, they thrilled
    through my breast
As swiftly as lightning leaps down from on
    high
When the chariot of God rolls along the
    black sky!
While his breath, floating round me, was soft
    as the breeze
That played in my tresses, and rustled the
    trees.

At last on my head a deep blessing he
    poured,
Then plumed his bright pinions, and upward
    he soared —
And up, up, he went, through the blue sky,
    so far,
He seemed to float there like a glittering
    star;

Yet still my eyes followed his radiant flight,
Till, lost in the azure, he passed from my sight.
Then, O how I feared, as I caught the last
    gleam
Of his vanishing form, it was only a dream —
When soft voices murmured once more from
    the tree,
'Come, brother, the angels are waiting for
    thee!'"

O, pale grew that mother, and heavy her
    heart,
For she knew her fair boy from this world
    must depart;
That his bright locks must fade in the dust
    of the tomb
Ere the autumn winds withered the sum-
    mer's rich bloom.
O, how his young footsteps she watched,
    day by day,
As his delicate form wasted slowly away,
Till the soft light of heaven seemed shed
    o'er his face,
And he crept up to die in her loving em-
    brace!
"O clasp me, dear mother, close, close to
    your breast!
On that gentle pillow again let me rest:

Let me once more gaze up in that dear lov-
    ing eye,
And then, O, methinks, I can willingly
    die.
Now kiss me, dear mother, O quickly, for
    see
The bright, blessed angels are waiting for
    me!"

O, wild was the anguish that swept through
    her breast
As the long, frantic kiss on his pale lips she
    pressed,
And felt the vain search of his soft, plead-
    ing eye
As it strove to meet hers ere the fair boy
    could die!
"I see you not, mother, for darkness and
    night
Are hiding your dear loving face from my
    sight;
But I hear your low sobbing: dear mother,
    good-bye!
The angels are ready to bear me on high.
I will wait for you there; but, O, tarry not
    long
Lest grief at your absence should sadden
    my song!"

He ceased, and his hands meekly clasped
    on his breast,
While his sweet face sank down on its pil-
    low of rest;
Then closing his eyes, now all rayless and
    dim,
He went up with the angels that waited for
    him.   *Caroline M. Sawyer.*

The Children's Hour.

BETWEEN the dark and the day-
    light,
    When the night is beginning to
      lower,
Comes a pause in the day's occupations
    That is known as the Children's Hour.

I hear in the chamber above me
    The patter of little feet,
The sound of a door that is opened,
    And voices soft and sweet.

From my study I see in the lamp-light,
    Descending the broad hall stair,
Grave Alice, and laughing Allegra,
    And Edith with golden hair.

A whisper, and then a silence ;
  Yet I know by their merry eyes
They are plotting and planning together
  To take me by surprise.

A sudden rush from the stairway,
  A sudden raid from the hall !
By three doors left unguarded
  They enter my castle wall !

They climb up into my turret
  O'er the arms and back of my chair;
If I try to escape, they surround me;
  They seem to be every-where.

They almost devour me with kisses;
  Their arms about me entwine,
Till I think of the Bishop of Bingen
  In his Mouse-Tower on the Rhine !

Do you think, O blue-eyed banditti,
  Because you have scaled the wall,
Such an old Moustache as I am
  Is not a match for you all !

I have you fast in my fortress,
  And will not let you depart,
But put you down in the dungeon,
  In the round-tower of my heart.

And there will I keep you forever,
  Yes, forever and a day,
Till the walls shall crumble to ruin,
  And molder in dust away!   *Longfellow.*

———————

The Beggar Girl.

VER the mountain and over the
      moor,
    Hungry and bare-foot, I wander
      forlorn;
My father is dead and my mother is poor,
  And she grieves for the days that will
      never return!

Pity, kind gentlefolk, friends of humanity;
  Cold blows the wind, and the night's
      coming on;
Give me some food for my mother, for
      charity;
  Give me some food, and I will be gone.

Call me not lazy, nor beggar, nor bold
      enough;
  Fain would I learn both to knit and to sew;
I 've two little brothers at home; when
      they 're old enough
  They will work hard for the gifts you
      bestow!

Think while you revel so careless and free,
  Secure from the wind, and well-clothéd
    and fed,
Should fortune so change it, how hard it
    would be
To beg at a door for a morsel of bread!

Pity, kind gentlefolk, friends of humanity,
  Cold blows the wind, and the night's
    coming on;
Give me some food for my mother, for
    charity;
Give me some food, and I will be gone.

————•————

Benny's Christmas.

HAD told him, Christmas morning,
    As he sat upon my knee
Holding fast his little stockings,
    Stuffed as full as full could be,
And attentive listening to me,
    With a face demure and mild,
That good Santa Claus, who filled them,
    Does not love a naughty child.

"But we'll be dood, wont we, modder,"
    And from off my lap he slid,
Digging deep among the *goodies*
    In his crimson stockings hid,

8

While I turned me to my table,
  Where a tempting goblet stood,
Brimming high with dainty egg-nog,
  Sent me by a neighbor good.

But the kitten, there before me,
  With his white paw, nothing loth,
Sat, by way of entertainment,
  Slapping off the shining froth:
And, in not the gentlest humor
  At the loss of such a treat,
I confess I rather rudely
  Thrust him out into the street.

Then how Benny's blue eyes kindled!
  Gathering up the precious store
He had busily been pouring
  In his tiny pinafore,
With a generous look that shamed me,
  Sprang he from the carpet bright,
Showing by his mien indignant
  All a baby's sense of right.

"Come back, Harney!" called he loudly,
  As he held his apron white;
"You sall have my candy wabbit!"
  But the door was fastened tight.

So he stood abashed and silent
   In the center of the floor,
With defeated look, alternate
   Bent, on me and on the door.

Then, as from a sudden impulse,
   Quickly ran he to the fire,
And, while eagerly his bright eyes
   Watched the flames go high and higher,
In a brave, clear key he shouted,
   Like some lordly little elf,
"Santa Taus! tum down de chimney;
   Make my modder 'have herself!"

"I will be a good girl, Benny,"
   Said I, feeling the reproof,
And straightway recalled poor Harney,
   Mewing on the gallery roof.
Soon the anger was forgotten,
   Laughter chased away the frown,
And they played beneath the live oaks
   Till the dusky night came down.

In my dim, fire-lighted chamber
   Harney purred beneath my chair,
And my play-worn boy beside me
   Knelt to say his evening prayer:

"Dod bess fader, Dod bess modder,
    Dod bess sister "— then a pause,
And the sweet young lips devoutly
    Murmured, " Dod bess Santa Taus ! "

He is sleeping — brown and silken
    Lie the lashes, long and meek,
Like caressing, clinging shadows,
    On his plump and peachy cheek.
And I bend above him, weeping
    Thankful tears — O undefiled !
For a woman's crown of glory,
    For the blessing of a child !

A Child's Thoughts of God.

HEY say that God lives very high !
But if you look above the pines
You cannot see our God.   And
    why ?

And if you dig down in the mines,
You never see him in the gold,
Though from him all its glory shines.

God is so good, he wears a fold
Of heaven and earth across his face—
Like secrets kept, for love untold :

But still I feel that his embrace
Slides down by thrills through all things
 made,
Through sight and sound of every place :

As if my tender mother laid
On my shut lids, her kisses' pressure,
Half-waking me at night; and said,
"Who kissed you through the dark, dear
 guesser?" *Elizabeth Barrett Browning.*

O HOLY is the sway
 Of that mysterious sense which bids us
 bend
Toward the young souls now clothed in
 helpless clay —
 Fragile beginnings of a mighty end —
 Angels unwinged — which human care
 must tend
Till they can tread the world's rough path
 alone,
 ·Serve for themselves, or in themselves
 offend.
But God o'erlooketh all from his high throne,
And sees with eyes benign their weakness
 and our own ! *Mrs. Norton.*

This Little Life.

LITTLE bird on a little tree
    Is singing a little song;
While a little sock, for my little boy,
    I am knitting by little along.

With a little crumb the little bird
    Its little birdie feeds;
A little bread and a little milk
    My little baby needs.

Then the little plans for these little ones
    With a little care are made,
And the little bird and the little babe
    In their little beds are laid.

To the little birdie's little nest
    Comes a little stray moonbeam;
To my little babie's little rest
    A little shining dream.

A little night and a little day
    Is peeping a little in,
And the little work and the little play
    Of the little world begin.

A little while, and the little bird
    Is singing its little song;
A little while, and my little sock
    I am knitting by little along.

Then the little crumbs and the little cares
  For the little bird and boy,
The little dreams and the little prayers
  The little day employ,—

Till, little by little, the song is sung;
And, little by little, the stitches strung;
And the little bird and the little wife
End, little by little, this little life.

                          Elizabeth O. Hoyt.

The Pauper Child's Burial.

STRETCHED on a rude plank the
    dead pauper lay;
    No weeping friends gathered to bear
    him away;
His white, slender fingers were clasped on
  his breast;
The pauper child meekly lay taking his
  rest.

The hair on his forehead was carelessly
  parted;
No one cared for him, the desolate-hearted:
In life none had loved him—his pathway,
  all sear,
Had not one sweet blossom its sadness to
  cheer.

No fond, gentle mother had ever caressed
him,
In tones of affection and tenderness blessed
him ;
For ere his eye greeted the light of the day,
His mother had passed in her anguish
away.

Poor little one ! often thy meek eyes have
sought
The smile of affection, of kindness un-
bought,
And wistfully gazing, in wond'ring surprise,
That no one beheld thee with pitying eyes.

And when in strange gladness thy young
voice was heard,
As in winter's stern sadness the song of the
bird,
Harsh voices rebuked thee, and, cow'ring
in fear,
Thy glad song was hushed in a sob and a
tear.

And when the last pang rent thy heartstrings
in twain,
And burst from thy bosom the last sign of
pain,

No gentle one soothed thee, in love's melt-
ing tone,
With fond arm around thee in tenderness
thrown.

Stern voices and cold mingled strange in
thine ear
With the song of the angels the dying may
hear;
And thrillingly tender, amid death's alarms,
Was thy mother's voice welcoming thee to
her arms.

Thy fragile form, wrapped in its coarse
shroud, reposes
In slumbers as sweet as if pillowed on roses;
And while on thy coffin the rude clods are
pressed,
The Good Shepherd folds the shorn lamb
to his breast.   *Mrs. Bailey.*

The New Moon.

DEAR mother, how pretty
The moon looks to-night!
She was never so cunning before;
Her two little horns
Are so sharp and so bright,
I hope she'll not grow any more.

If I were up there,
With you and my friends,
I 'd rock in it nicely, you 'd see;
I 'd sit in the middle
And hold by both ends;
O, what a bright cradle 't would be!

I would call to the stars
To keep out of the way,
Lest we should rock over their toes;
And then I would rock
Till the dawn of the day,
And see where the pretty moon goes.

And there we would stay
In the beautiful skies,
And through the bright clouds we would
roam;
We would see the sun set,
And see the sun rise,
And on the next rainbow come home.

Mrs. Follen.

———————◆———————

TAKE care of the children.   Nor wasted
Is care on the weakest of these;
The culturer the product has tasted,
And found it the palate to please.

There are sheaves pushed higher and faster,
    And age has more branches and roots;
But dearer are none to the Master
    Than childhood, in blossoms and fruits!
                    W. B. Tappan.

Ode to A Son.

THOU happy, happy elf!
    (But stop, first let me kiss away that
           tear—)
    Thou tiny image of myself!
(My love, he's poking peas into his ear!)
    Thou merry, laughing sprite!
    With spirits feather-light,
Untouched by sorrow, and unsoiled by sin,—
(Good heavens! the child is swallowing a
      pin!)
    Thou cherub-brat of earth!
Fit playfellow for fays, by moonlight pale,
    In harmless sport and mirth!
(That dog will bite him if he pulls his tail!)
    *   *   *   *   *
Fresh as the morn, and brilliant as its star—
(I wish that window had an iron bar—)
Bold as the hawk, yet gentle as the dove—
    (I tell you what, my love,
I cannot write, unless he's sent above.)

Under the Snow.

UR baby lies under the snow, sweet
wife, our baby lies under the snow,
Out in the dark with the night, while
the winds so loudly blow;
As a dead saint thou art pale, sweet wife,
and the cross is on thy breast;
O, the snow no more can chill that little
dove in its nest!

Shall we shut the baby out, sweet wife, while
the chilling winds do blow?
O, the grave is now its bed, and its coverlet
is of snow.
O, our merry bird is snared, sweet wife, that
a rain of music gave,
And the snow falls on our hearts, and our
hearts are each a grave!

O, it was the lamp of life, sweet wife, blown
out in a night of gloom,
A leaf from our flower of love, nipped in its
fresh spring bloom:
But the lamp will shine above, sweet wife,
and the leaf again shall grow,
Where there are no bitter winds, and no
dreary, dreary snow!   *Chadwick.*

The Golden Stair.

UT away the little dresses
  That the darling used to wear;
She will need them on earth never;
  She has climbed the golden stair;
She is happy with the angels,
  And I long for her sweet kiss,
Where her little feet are waiting
  In the realm of perfect bliss.

Lay aside her little playthings,
  Wet with mother's pearly tears;
How we shall miss little Nellie
  All the coming weary years!
Fold the dainty little dresses
  That she never more will wear,
For her little feet are waiting
  Up above the golden stair.

Kiss the little curly tresses
  Cut from her bright golden hair,—
Do the angels kiss our darling
  In the realm so bright and fair?
O! we pray to meet our darling
  For a long, long, sweet embrace,
Where the little feet are waiting,—
  There we'll meet her face to face.

Who Are You?

"WHO are you? who are you?
Little boy, that's running after
Every one up and down,
Mingling   sighing   with   your
laughter?"
"I am Cupid, lady belle;
I am Cupid, and no other."
"Little boy, then pr'ythee tell
How is Venus? — *How's your mother?* ·
Little boy, little boy,
I desire you tell me true.
Cupid, O, you're altered so!
No wonder I cry, *Who are you?*

"Who are you? who are you?
Little boy, where is your bow?
You had a bow, my little boy ——"
"So had your mamma,—long ago."
"Little boy, where is your torch?"
"Madam, I have given it up:
Torches are no use at all;
Hearts will never now *flare up.*"
"Naughty boy, naughty boy,
Such words as these I never knew.
Cupid, O, you're altered so!
No wonder I say, *Who are you?*"

Little Nell.

PRING, with breezes cool and airy,
Opened on a little fairy:
Ever restless, making merry,
She, with pouting lips of cherry,
Lisped the words she could not master,
Vexed that she might speak no faster.
Laughing, running, playing, dancing,
Mischief all her joys enhancing,
Full of baby-mirth and glee,
It was a joyous sight to see
      Sweet little Nell!

Summer came, the green earth's lover,
Ripening the tufted clover,
Calling down the glittering showers,
Breathing on the buds and flowers —
Rivaling young pleasant May
In a generous holiday.
Smallest insects hummed a tune
Through the blessed nights of June,
And the maiden sang the song
Through the days so bright and long —
      Dear little Nell!

Autumn came; the flowers were falling —
Death the little one was calling;

Pale and wan she grew, and weakly,
Bearing all her pains so meekly
That to us she seemed still dearer
As the trial-hour drew nearer.
But she left us hopeless, lonely,
Watching by her semblance only :
And a little grave they made her ;
In the church-yard cold they laid her —
Laid her softly down to rest
With a white rose on her breast —
    Poor little Nell !

A Farewell.

Y fairest child, I have no song to
    give you ;
No lark could pipe to skies so dull
    and gray ;
Yet, ere we part, one lesson I can leave you
    For every day.

Be good, sweet maid, and let who will be
    clever ;
Do noble things, not dream them, all day
    long ;
And so make life, death, and that vast for-
    ever
    One grand, sweet song.

The Angels' Whisper.

[Some indulge in the superstition that when a child smiles in its sleep it is "talking with angels."]

BABY was sleeping;
Its mother was weeping,
For her husband was far on the
wild, raging sea,
And the tempest was swelling
Round the fisherman's dwelling,
And she cried, "Dermot, darling, O come
back to me!"

Her beads while she numbered,
The baby still slumbered,
And smiled in her face as she bended her
knee;
"O, blest be that warning,
My child, thy sleep adorning,
For I know that the angels are whispering
with thee.

"And while they are keeping
Bright watch o'er thy sleeping,
O pray to them softly, my baby, with me!
And say thou wouldst rather
They'd watch o'er thy father!
For I know that the angels are whispering
with thee."

9

The dawn of the morning
Saw Dermot returning,
And the wife wept with joy her babe's father
to see;
And closely caressing
Her child, with a blessing,
Said, "I knew that the angels were whis-
pering with thee."
Samuel Lover.

Alone in the Dark.

STAY by me to-night, dear mamma,"
said a child;
"The rain rattles down, and the
wind is so wild;
I shut up my eyes, and I cover my head,
And draw myself up in a heap in the bed,
And I think about robbers, and shiver with
fear —
Do stay by me, mother! It is so dark up
here."

"I cannot, my darling; and why should I
stay?
You are never afraid to come up here by day;
You study and play in this same little room,
And never have left it with fear or with
gloom;

Why, then, when you 're wrapped up so cosy
    and warm,
Do you think about things that can do you
    no harm ? "

" O, mother, it 's light in the daytime, you
    know,
And the sunshine then puts all the room in
    a glow ;
And up from the hall comes a murmur of
    sound,
Where Jennie and Kittie are running
    around ;
And though your voice, dear mother, I do n't
    always hear,
Yet it 's so light and cheerful, *I know you
are there.*"

" My dear little boy, I 'm afraid you forget
That God is near by, watching over my pet.
Nor darkness nor light would be safe with-
    out One
Who sees us and guards us till life's race is
    run.
In the loneliest night he is close by your
    side ;
If you love him and trust him, ' The Lord
    will provide.'

" You never need fear, but when feeble and
faint
Then call upon God, who will hear your
complaint.
There 's no one to hurt you when God is so
nigh ;
His angels, to keep you, descend from the
sky."

The child put his little soft hand in her own,
And kissed the sweet face that so lovingly
shone :
" You may put out the light, mother dear,
when you please ;
If I feel afraid now, I will think *that God
sees.*"

M. E. M.

Ouη Wee White Rose.

ALL in our marriage garden
Grew, smiling, smiling **up to**
God,
A bonnier flower than ever
Sucked the green warmth of the sod ;
O beautiful unfathomably
Its little life unfurled ;
And crown of all things was our wee
White Rose, of all the world.

From out a balmy bosom
  Our bud of beauty grew;
It fed on smiles for sunshine,
  On tears for daintier dew.
Aye, nestling warm and tenderly,
  Our leaves of love were curled
So close and close about our wee
  White Rose, of all the world.

With mystical, faint fragrance
  Our house of life she filled —
Revealed each hour some fairy tower
  Where wingéd hopes might build!
We saw — though none like us might
    see —
Such precious promise pearled
Upon the petals of our wee
  White Rose, of all the world.

But evermore the halo
  Of angel-light increased,
Like the mystery of moonlight
  That folds some fairy feast.
Snow-white, snow-soft, snow-silently,
  Our darling bud up-curled,
And dropped i' the grave — God's lap —
    our wee
  White Rose, of all the world.

Our Rose was but in blossom;
   Our life was but in spring;
When down the solemh midnight
   We heard the spirits sing —
' " Another bud of infancy
   With holy dews impearled!"
And in their hands they bore our wee
   White Rose, of all the world.

You scarce could think so small a thing
   Could leave a loss so large;
Her little light such shadow fling
   From dawn to sunset's marge.
In other springs our life may be
   In bannered bloom unfurled,
But never, never match our wee
   White Rose, of all the world.

Massey.

My First-Born.

E sha'n't be their namesake; the rather
   That both are such opulent men :
His name shall be that of his father,
   My Benjamin — shortened to Ben.

"Yes, Ben, though it cost him a portion
   In each of my relative's wills,
I scorn such baptismal extortion —
   (That creaking of boots must be Squills.)

" It is clear, though his means may be narrow,
 This infant his age will adorn;
I shall send him to Oxford from Harrow,—
 I wonder how soon he'll be born!"

A spouse thus was airing his fancies
 Below — 't was a labor of love,—
And calmly reflecting on Nancy's
 More practical labor above;

Yet while it so pleased him to ponder,
 Elated, at ease, and alone,
That pale, patient victim up yonder,
 Had budding delights of her own;

Sweet thoughts, in their essence diviner
 Than paltry ambition and pelf;
A cherub, no babe will be finer,
 Invented and nursed by herself.

One breakfasting, dining, and teaing,
 With appetite naught can appease,
And quite a young reasoning being
 When called on to yawn and to sneeze.

What cares that heart, trusting and tender,
 For fame or aruncular wills?
Except for the name and the gender,
 She is almost as tranquil as Squills.

That father, in revery centered,
  Dumbfounded, his thoughts in a whirl,
Heard Squills, as the creaking boots en-
    tered,
  Announce that his Boy was — a Girl!
                              Frederick Locker.

The Patter of Little Feet.

P with the sun at morning,
    Away to the garden he hies,
  To see if the sleepy blossoms
    Have begun to open their eyes;
  Running a race with the wind,
    His step as light and fleet,
  Under my window I hear
    The patter of little feet.

Anon to the brook he wanders,
    In swift and noiseless flight,
  Splashing the sparkling ripples
    Like a fairy water-sprite.
  No sand under fabled river
    Has gleams like his golden hair;
  No pearly sea-shell is fairer
    Than his slender ankles bare;

Nor the rosiest stem of coral,
   That blushes in Ocean's bed,
Is sweet as the flush that follows
   Our darling's airy tread.

From a broad window my neighbor
   Looks down on our little cot,
And watches the "poor man's bless-
      ing;"
   I cannot envy his lot:
He has pictures, books, and music,
   Bright fountains, and noble trees,
Flowers that blossom in vases,
   Birds from beyond the seas;
But never does childish laughter
   His homeward footsteps greet;
His stately halls ne'er echo
   The tread of innocent feet.

This child is our "speaking picture,"
   A birdling that chatters and sings,
Sometimes a "sleeping cherub,"—
   Our other one has wings;—
His heart is a charméd casket,
   Full of all that's cunning and sweet,
And no harpstrings hold such music
   As follows his twinkling feet.

When the glory of sunset opens
　　The highway by angels trod,
And seems to unbar the City
　　Whose builder and maker is God,
Close to the crystal portal,
　　I see by the gates of pearl,
The eyes of our other angel —
　　A twin-born little girl.

And I ask to be taught and directed
　　To guide his footsteps aright,
So that I be accounted worthy
　· To walk in sandals of light;
And hear, amid songs of welcome
　　From messengers trusty and fleet,
On the starry floor of heaven,
　　The patter of little feet.

Sarah E. Wallace.

Life's Lessons.

HASING after butterflies, hunting
　　after flowers,
Listening to the wild birds through
　　the sunny hours;
Looking up the hens' nests on the fragrant
　mows,
Tending to the lambkins, driving ·up the
　cows;

Mixing play and labor in my childish glee,
Learned I life's first lesson — learned I to
be free.

Waving on the tree-tops, roaming o'er the
. hills,
Wandering through the meadows, fishing in
the rills,
Floating on the rivers, riding o'er the plains,
Plodding through the corn-fields, dropping
golden grains,
Mixing play and labor with a childish glee,
Learned I life's first lesson — learned I to
be free.

Laughing 'mong the green leaves as the ripe
fruit fell;
Gathering the brown nuts in the woody dell;
Tripping at the spinning-wheel, ever to and
fro;
Dancing at the paring-bee on a merry toe;
Mixing play and labor with a youthful glee,
Learned I life's first lesson — learned I to
be free.

Singing o'er my milk pail while the dews
were bright,
Toiling in the dairy with a spirit light,

Using mop and duster, washboard, oven,
　　broom,
Scissors, thread and needle, as might chance
　　to come ;
Mixing play and labor, ever cheerfully,
Learned I life's best lessons — learned I to
　　be free.

Conning these best lessons, poring over
　　books,
Dreaming of the future in the quiet nooks;
Gleaning, ever gleaning, as the days went
　　by,
Thinking, never shrinking, not afraid to try ;
Mixing play and labor, ever joyously,
Learned I life's great lessons — learned I to
　　be free.　　　　　　　　*Frances D. Gage.*

The Ballad of Babie Bell.

HAVE you not heard the poets tell
　　How came the dainty Babie Bell
　　　Into this world of ours?
　　The gates of heaven were left ajar :
With folded hands and dreamy eyes,
Wandering out of Paradise,
She saw this planet, like a star,
Hung in the glistening depths of even —

Its bridges, running to and fro,
O'er which the white-winged angels go,
Bearing the holy dead to heaven !
She touched a bridge of flowers — those feet,
So light they did not bend the bells
Of the celestial asphodels,
They fell like dew upon the flowers —
Then all the air grew strangely sweet !
And thus came dainty Babie Bell
Into this world of ours.

She came, and brought delicious May.
The swallows built beneath the eaves ;
Like sunlight in and out the leaves
The robins went the livelong day ;
The lily swung its noiseless bell,
And o'er the porch the trembling vine
Seemed bursting with its veins of wine :
How sweetly, softly, twilight fell !
O, earth was full of singing birds,
And opening spring-tide flowers,
When the dainty Babie Bell
Came to this world of ours !

O Babie, dainty Babie Bell,
How fair she grew from day to day !
What woman-nature filled her eyes,
What poetry within them lay !

Those dark and tender twilight eyes,
  So full of meaning, pure and bright
  As if she yet stood in the light
Of those open gates of Paradise !

And so we loved her more and more :
Ah, never in our hearts before
  Was love so lovely born !
We felt we had a link between
This real world and that unseen —
  The land beyond the morn !
And for the love of those dear eyes,
  For love of her whom God let forth
  (The mother's being ceased on earth
When Babie came from Paradise) —
For love of Him who smote our lives,
  And woke the chords of joy and pain,
We said, " Dear Christ ! "—our hearts bent
      down
  . Like violets after rain.

And now the orchards, which were white
  And red with blossoms when she came,
Were rich in autumn's mellow prime :
  The clustered apples burned like flame,
The soft-cheeked peaches blushed and fell,
The ivory chestnut burst its shell,

The grapes hung purpling in the grange :
And time wrought just as rich a change
In little Babie Bell.

Her lissome form more perfect grew,
   And in her features we could trace,
   In softened curves, her mother's face !
Her angel-nature ripened too.
We thought her lovely when she came,
   But she was holy, saintly now :
   Around her pale angelic brow
We saw a slender ring of flame.

God's hand had taken away the seal
   That held the portals of her speech ;
And oft she said a few strange words
   Whose meaning lay beyond our reach.
She never was a child to us ;
   We never held her being's key :
We could not teach her holy things —
   She was Christ's self in purity.

It came upon us by degrees :
   We saw its shadow ere it fell —
The knowledge that our God had sent
   His messenger for Babie Bell.

We shuddered with unlanguaged pain,
  And all our hopes were changed to fears,
  And all our thoughts ran into tears,
    Like sunshine into rain.
We cried aloud in our belief,
  "O, smite us gently, gently, God!
  Teach us to bend and kiss the rod,
And perfect grow through grief."
    Ah, how we loved her, God can tell;
Her heart was folded deep in ours;
    Our hearts are broken, Babie Bell!

At last he came, the messenger,
  The messenger from unseen lands!
And what did dainty Babie Bell?
  She only crossed her little hands;
She only looked more meek and fair!
We parted back her silken hair;
We wove the roses round her brow,
White buds, the summer's drifted snow—
  Wrapped her from head to foot in
    flowers:
And thus went dainty Babie Bell
  Out of this world of ours!
                    Thomas B. Aldrich.

Little Mamie.

SLEEP on, fair babe, beneath thy
    mother's smile;
No fear hast thou of sin, nor thought
    of guile.
Sleep on; nor let the curtains of thine eyes
In hasty wakefulness or fright arise.
O skin, so like the roseate tinted pearl!
O hair, in whose soft silk we trace a curl!
O limbs, reclining in such lines of grace!
O dainty robes of linen fine and lace!
O baby form! so like an angel given,
Thou prov'st to earth the purity of heaven.
We know not what thy future life may be,
What joys may thrill, what griefs encircle,
    thee;
Yet *this* we know, aught more we cannot
    tell:
That God is love. He doeth all things
    well.   *Rachel A. Smith.*

Thy days, my little one, were few:
    An angel's morning visit,
That came and vanished with the dew—
    'T was here; 't is gone; where is it?
Yet didst thou leave behind thee
A clue for love to find thee.
             Montgomery.

10

Where Did You Come From, Baby?

"WHERE did you come from, baby
dear?"
"Out of the every-where into the
here."

"Where did you get your eyes so blue?"
"Out of the sky as I came through."

"What makes the light in them sparkle and
spin?"
"Some of the starry spikes left in."

"Where did you get that little tear?"
"I found it waiting when I got here."

"What makes your forehead so smooth and
high?"
"A soft hand stroked it as I went by."

"What makes your cheek like a warm white
rose?"
"Something better than any one knows."

"Whence that three-cornered smile of bliss?"
"Three angels gave me at once a kiss."

"Where did you get that pearly ear?"
"God spoke, and it came out to hear."

"Where did you get those arms and hands?"
"Love made itself into hooks and bands."

"Feet, whence did you come, you darling
    things?"
"From the same body as the cherub's
    wings."

"How did they all just come to be you?"
"God thought about me, and so I grew."

"But how did you come to us, you dear?"
"God thought of you, and so I am here."

George Macdonald.

Under My Window.

UNDER my window, under my win-
    dow,
    All the midsummer weather,
    Three little girls, with fluttering
      curls,
  Flit to and fro together: —
There's Belle, with her bonnet of satin
    sheen,
And Maud, with her mantle of silver-
    green,
    And Kate, with her scarlet feather.

Under my window, under my window,
  Leaning stealthily over,
Merry and clear the voice I hear
  Of each glad-hearted rover.
Ah! sly little Kate, she steals my roses,
And Maud and Belle twine wreaths and
    posies,
  As busy as bees in clover.

Under my window, under my window,
  In the blue midsummer weather,
Stealing slow, on a hushed tip-toe,
  I catch them all together : —
Belle, with her bonnet of satin sheen,
And Maud, with her mantle of silver-green,
  And Kate, with her scarlet feather.

Under my window, under my window,
  And off through the orchard closes;
While Maud, she flouts, and Belle, she pouts,
  They scamper, and drop their posies.
But dear little Kate takes naught amiss,
And leaps in my arms with a loving kiss,
  And I give her all my roses.
              T. Westwood.

The Little Brother.

AMONG the beautiful pictures
 That hang on Memory's wall,
Is one of a dim old forest,
 That seemeth the best of all;
Not for its gnarled oaks olden,
 Dark with the misletoe;
Not for the violets golden
 That sprinkle·the vale below;
Not for the milk-white lilies
 That lean from the fragrant hedge,
Coquetting all day with the sunbeams,
 And stealing their golden edge;
Not for the vines on the upland
 Where the bright red berries rest;
Nor the pinks, nor the pale, sweet cowslip,
 It seemeth to me the best.

I once had a little brother,
 With eyes that were dark and deep:
In the lap of that olden forest
 He lieth in peace asleep.
Light as the down of the thistle,
 Free as the winds that blow,
We roved there the beautiful summers,
 The summers of long ago.

But his feet on the hills grew weary;
　And one of the autumn eves
I made for my little brother
　A bed of the yellow leaves.

Sweetly his pale arms folded
　My neck in a meek embrace,
As the light of immortal beauty
　Silently covered his face;
And when the arrows of sunset
　Lodged in the tree-tops bright,
He fell, in his saint-like beauty,
　Asleep by the gates of light.
Therefore, of all the pictures
　That hang on Memory's wall,
The one of the dim old forest
　Seemeth the best of all.

Alice Carey.

The Pet Lamb.

HE dew was falling fast, the stars
　began to blink;
　I heard a voice; it said, "Drink,
　pretty creature, drink!"
And, looking o'er a hedge, before me I
　espied
A snow-white mountain-lamb with a maiden
　at its side.

Nor sheep nor kine were near; the lamb was
    all alone,
And by a slender cord was tethered to a
    stone;
With one knee on the grass did the little
    maiden kneel,
While to that mountain-lamb she gave its
    evening meal.

The lamb, while from her hand he thus his
    supper took,
Seemed to feast with head and ears, and
    his tail with pleasure shook.
"Drink, pretty creature, drink!" she said
    in such a tone,
That I almost received her heart into my
    own.

'T was little Barbara Lewthwaite, a child of
    beauty rare :—
I watched them with delight; they were a
    lovely pair.—
Now with her empty can the maiden turned
    away;
But ere ten yards were gone, her footsteps
    did she stay.

Right toward the lamb she looked, and from
    a shady place
I, unobserved, could see the workings of her
    face.
If Nature to her tongue could measured
    numbers bring,
Thus, thought I, to her lamb that little maid
    might sing:

"What ails thee, young one? What? Why
    pull so at thy cord?
Is it not well with thee? well for both bed
    and board?
Thy plot of grass is soft, and green as grass
    can be;
Rest, little young one, rest; what is 't that
    aileth thee?

"What is it thou wouldst seek? What is
    wanting to thy heart?
Thy limbs, are they not strong? And
    beautiful thou art.
This grass is tender grass; these flowers
    they have no peers;
And that green corn all day is rustling in
    thy ears.

" If the sun be shining hot, do but stretch
    thy woolen chain —
This beech is standing by, its covert thou
    canst gain ;
For rain and mountain-storms — the like
    thou needst not fear ;
The rain and storm are things that scarcely
    can come here.

" Rest, little young·one, rest ; thou hast for-
    got the day
When my father found thee first in places far
    away ;
Many flocks were on the hills, but thou wert
    owned by none,
And thy mother from thy side for evermore
    was gone.

" He took thee in his arms, and in pity
    brought thee home ;
A blessed day for thee ! Then whither
    wouldst thou roam ?
A faithful nurse thou hast — the dam that
    did thee yean
Upon the mountain-tops — no kinder could
    have been.

" Thou know'st that twice a day I have
 brought thee in this can
Fresh water from the brook, as clear as
 ever ran ;
And twice in the day, when the ground is
 wet with dew,
I bring thee draughts of milk — warm milk
 it is, and new.

" Thy limbs will shortly be twice stout as
 they are now ;
Then I 'll yoke thee to my cart, like a pony
 to the plow,
My playmate thou shalt be ; and when the
 wind is cold,
Our hearth shall be thy bed, our house shall
 be thy fold.

" It will not, will not rest ! Poor creature,
 can it be
That 't is thy mother's heart which is work-
 ing so in thee ?
Things that I know not of belike to thee
 are dear,
And dreams of things which thou canst
 neither see nor hear.

"Alas, the mountain-tops that look so green
    and fair!
I've heard of fearful winds and darkness
    that come there;
The little brooks, that seem all pastime and
    all play,
When they are angry roar like lions for
    their prey.

"Here thou needst not dread the raven in
    the sky;
Night and day thou art safe — our cottage
    is hard by.
Why bleat so after me? Why pull so at thy
    chain?
Sleep, and at break of day I will come to
    thee again."

As homeward through the lane I went with
    lazy feet,
This song to myself did I oftentimes re-
    peat;
And it seemed, as I retraced the ballad, line
    by line,
That but half of it was hers, and one half
    of it was mine.

Again, and once again, did I repeat the
    song;
"Nay," said I, "more than half to the dam-
    sel must belong,
For she looked with such a look, and she
    spake with such a tone,
That I almost received her heart into my
    own."   *Wordsworth.*

———————

Wishing.—A Child's Song.

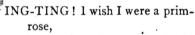

RING-TING! I wish I were a prim-
    rose,
  A bright yellow primrose blowing in
    the Spring;
  The stooping boughs above me,
  The wandering bee to love me,
The fern and moss to creep across,
  And the elm-tree for our king!
  Nay, stay! I wish I were an elm-tree,
A great, lofty elm-tree, with green leaves
    gay!
  The winds would set them dancing,
  The sun and moonshine glance in,
The birds would house among the boughs,
  And sweetly sing.

O, no! I wish I were a robin,
A robin or a little wren, every-where to go;
  Through forest, field, or garden,
  And ask no leave or pardon,
Till winter comes with icy thumbs
  To ruffle up our wing!
  Well, tell! Where should I fly to,
Where go to sleep in the dark wood or dell?
  Before a day was over,
  Home comes the rover
For mother's kiss — sweeter this
  Than any other thing.

William Allingham.

The Afternoon Nap.

HE farmer sat in his easy-chair,
  Smoking his pipe of clay,
While his hale old wife, with busy care,
  Was clearing the dinner away;
A sweet little girl, with fine blue eyes,
On her grandfather's knee was catching
  flies.

The old man laid his hand on her head,
  With a tear on his wrinkled face;
He thought how often her mother, dead,
  Had sat in the self-same place;

And a tear stole down from his half-shut-
    eye;
"Don't smoke!" said the child, "how it
    makes you cry!"

The house-dog lay stretched out on the floor,
    Where the shade after noon used to steal;
The busy old wife, by the open door,
    Was turning the spinning-wheel;
And the old brass clock on the mantel-tree
Had plodded along to almost three;

Still the farmer sat in his easy-chair,
    While, close to his heaving breast,
The moistened brow and the cheek so fair
    Of his sweet grandchild were pressed;
His head bent down on her soft hair, lay:
Fast asleep were they both that summer
    day.   *Charles G. Eastman.*

Little Eyes and Little Hands.

LITTLE eyes,
    Like the shining blue above,
    Full of light and love,
        Full of glee;
Telling of a life within,
    In a world of sin,
        Born to you and me!

Will they see the golden way
Leading up to day?
And the God to whom we pray
 In the skies?

 Little hands,
In the long and weary strife
Of a toiling life,
 Will they win?
Will they early learn to bless?
Rescue from distress?
 Will they fear to sin?
For the true, the good, the right,
Will they bravely fight?
Strew along the paths of night
 Golden sands?

 Little feet,
Entered on a thorny way;
Will it lead to day
 And renown?
As its rugged steps are trod,
Will they climb to God
 And a seraph's crown?
Where the loving Saviour goes,
Finding friends or foes,
Will they follow, till life's close,
 As is meet?

Little eyes,
May they wear an angel's guise
In the upper skies!
Little hands,
May they, doing God's commands,
Rest in fairer lands!
May these little feet
Thee, dear Saviour, run to meet
At thy mercy-seat;
And with joy for sins forgiven,
Press to heaven!

The Real Prayer.—A Fact.

STOOD within a shadowy-aisled
Cathedral, vast and dim,
And listened to the organ's tone
Like a perpetual hymn.
'T was not the time for service grand,
When thousands gather there —
Only a few, with stricken hearts,
Bent low in silent prayer.

The pictures on the walls were works
Of some great master-hand,
And bade the solemn past return,
Like famed magician's wand.

And what a heaven was in the eye
  And face, upturned, divine,
Of that Madonna! Could one help
  But bow at *such* a shrine?

And O, the agony of Him —
  The Christ upon the tree!
I turned away — too much, too much
  Like stern reality.
And saint and martyr, bearing rack
  And torture for " His sake,"
O'er all the walls — enough it seemed
  The heart well-nigh to break.

I looked again at those in prayer,
  And said, Who knows the heart?
Those pictures — like reality —
  Are but the works of art.
And may not these be pictured prayers,
  The essence passed away —
Devotion's form without the soul,
  These worshipers to-day? "

I paused in thought, and said, " Thy *soul*,
  Religion, tell me where? "
When through the opened door there
    came
  An answer to my prayer.
11

A ragged little errand boy,
  With bundle in his hand,
Walked silently and knelt him down
  Where I had dared to stand.

He dropped the bundle by his side,
  And crossed his hands in prayer,
And lifted up his little face
  A *living picture* there.
And what an earnest, speaking face!
  How eloquent the form!
Face, form, and ragged garments said,
  " God shield me from the storm."

Madonna, saint, and martyr face
  Faded like mist away;
" The past be with the past," I said,
  " Devotion lives to-day."
That look of earnest, trusting faith
  No *hypocrite* may wear;
This poor, lone, friendless, kneeling
      child —
  The very soul of prayer.

Day after day I 've seen them kneel;
  Long prayers I 've often heard;
But never one like that to me —
  That prayer without a word.

And when I weary of the guilt
    That in devotions share,
I think of that young worshiper,
    And still keep faith in prayer.
                    Miss A. W. Sprague.

My Bird.

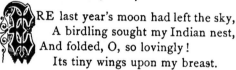

RE last year's moon had left the sky,
    A birdling sought my Indian nest,
And folded, O, so lovingly!
    Its tiny wings upon my breast.

From morn till evening's purple tinge,
    In winsome helplessness she lies;
Two rose-leaves, with a silken fringe,
    Shut softly on her starry eyes.

There's not in Ind a lovelier bird;
    Broad earth owns not a happier nest;
O God, thou hast a fountain stirred,
    Whose waters never more shall rest!

This beautiful, mysterious thing,
    This seeming visitant from heaven,
This bird with the immortal wing,
    To me — to me thy hand has given.

The pulse first caught its tiny stroke,
  The blood its crimson hue, from mine;
This life, which I have dared invoke,
  Henceforth is parallel with Thine.

A silent awe is in my room —
  I tremble with delicious fear;
The future, with its light and gloom,
  Time and eternity, are here.

Doubts, hopes, in eager tumult rise;
  Hear, O my God! one earnest prayer:
Room for my bird in paradise,
  And give her angel plumage there!
                          Mrs. Judson.

Cloud Pictures.

THE sun was fast sinking adown the
      west,
  The bees and the birds were seek-
      ing their rest,
As a family group, on the lawn at play,
Were whiling the evening hours away
The eldest, a rosy-cheeked, laughing girl,
Cried out, as she twined a golden curl,
"O see in the clouds! what a lovely hue!
How well it accords with the sky of blue!"

I mean to contrive, ere our next *soirée*,
A dress that will mingle those tints so gay.
Just look at that cloud! Do you not per-
    ceive
That it curves in the shape of my last new
    sleeve?"
"Why, Cora!" exclaimed, in a chiding tone,
A dreamy-eyed boy who had sat alone;
"I see but white angels amid the clouds;
They hover together in loving crowds
About the wide gates of yon paradise,
Whose glory shines through with such brill-
    iant dyes."
"Now *I* see the tunninest 'ittle doll,
Wis apron, and bonnet, and shoes, and all,"
Said sweet Baby Kitty, the pet and the pride,
As she gazed on the vapor-flecked heavens
    wide.
But Charlie, whose thoughts and ambition
    led
To wars and fierce battles of heroes, said,
"Ah! there is a battlement proud 'and
    strong:
But soldiers nor cannon will hold it long,
For see the armed host in those azure fields,
With a leader that perishes, ere he yields.
O! *these* are the pictures the clouds give me;
No dresses, nor angels, nor dolls, *I* see."

Then answered his mother, in accents mild,
" 'T is ever the same through our lives, my
    child :
Each one forms his pictures with fancy's art,
And paints them with feelings of mind and
    heart.
In all the vast clouds of events, my boy,
You 'll form either pictures of grief or joy.
Then strive e'er to keep in your fresh young
    soul
Such colors as shall, when events unroll,
Transfer to their shapes the soft tints of
    peace,
Till painting, and fancy, and life shall cease."

Rachel A. Smith.

Elsie Gathering Flowers.

ND as she gathered them
    She wondered more and more
    Who was the Master of the flowers,
    And made them grow
Out of the cold, dark earth.
" In my heart," she said,
" I love him ; and for him
Would leave my father's palace,
To labor in his garden."

Longfellow.

Baby Paul.

P in the early morning,
    Just at the peep of day,
  Driving the sleep from my eyelids,
    Pulling the quilts away;
Pinching my cheek and my forehead
  With his white fingers small,
This is my bright-eyed darling,
  This is my Baby Paul.

Down on the floor in the parlor,
  Creeping with laugh and shout,
Or, out in the kitchen and pantry,
  Tossing the things about;
Rattling the pans and the kettles,
  Scratching the table and wall,
This is my roguish darling,
  This is my Baby Paul.

Riding on papa's shoulder,
  Trotting on grandpa's knee,
Pulling his hair and whiskers,
  Laughing in wildest glee;
Reaching for grandma's knitting,
  Snatching her thimble and ball,
This is our household idol,
  This is our Baby Paul.

Playing bo-peep with his brother,
  Kissing the little girls,
Romping with aunt and uncles,
  Clutching his sister's curls;
Teasing old puss from his slumbers,
  Pattering o'er porch and hall,
This is our bonnie wee darling,
  This is our Baby Paul.

Nestling close up to my bosom,
  Laying his cheek to mine,
Covering my mouth with his kisses,
  Sweeter than golden wine;
Flinging his white arms about me,
  Soft as the snow-flakes fall,
This is my cherished darling,
  This is my Baby Paul.

Fair is his face as the lily's,
  Black are his eyes as the crows,
Sweet is his voice as the robin's,
  Red are his lips as the rose;
Bright is his smile as the sunbeams,
  Beaming when e'er I call,
This is my beautiful darling,
  This is my Baby Paul.

Dearer, a thousand times dearer,
  The wealth in my darling I hold,
Than all this earth's glittering treasure,
  Its glory, and honors, and gold;
If these at my feet were now lying,
  I'd gladly renounce them all
For the sake of my bright-eyed darling,
  My dear little Baby Paul.
                    Mrs. Bishop Thomson.

Mamma's Kisses.

KISS when I wake in the morning,
  A kiss when I go to bed;
A kiss when I burn my fingers,
  A kiss when I bump my head;

A kiss when my bath is over,
  A kiss when my bath begins;
My mamma is full of kisses —
  As full as nurse is of pins.

A kiss when I play with rattle,
  A kiss when I pull her hair;
She covered me over with kisses
  The day I fell from the stair.

A kiss when I give her trouble,
    A kiss when I give her joy;
There's nothing like mamma's kisses
    To her own little baby boy.

"Jack and Me."

ERE y' are—? Black your boots,
    boss?
    Do it for just five cents;
    Shine 'em up in a minute,
        That is, if nothin' prevents.

Set your foot right on there, sir;
    The mornin's kinder cold—
Sorter rough on a feller
    When his coat's a gittin' old.

Well, yes; call it a coat, sir;
    Though 'taint much more 'n a tear;
Can't get myself another—
    Aint got the stamps to spare.

Make as much as most on 'em—
    That's so; but then, you see,
They've only got one to do for,
    There's *two* on us—Jack and me.

Him? Why — that little feller,
　With a double-up sorter back,
Sittin' there on the gratin'
　Sunnin' hisself — that's Jack.

Used to be round sellin' papers;
　The cars, there, was his lay;
But he got shoved off the platform
　Under the wheels, one day.

Yes, the conductor did it —
　Gave him a regular throw —
He did n't care if he killed him;
　Some on 'em is just so.

He 's never been all right since, sir;
　Sorter quiet and queer;
Him, and me go together;
　He 's what they call cashier.

High old style for a boot-black!
　Made all the fellers laugh.
Jack and me had to take it;
　But we do n't mind no chaff.

Trouble? I guess not much, sir;
　Sometimes, when biz gets slack,
I do n't know how I 'd stand it
　If it was n't for little Jack.

Why, boss, you ought to hear him :
He says we need n't care
How rough luck is down here, sir,
If some day we get up *there.*

All done now! How's that, sir?
Shine like a pair o' lamps;
Mornin'— give it to Jack, sir,
He looks out for the stamps.

Children.

LIKE an isle of green and gladness
In the desert wild,
In our home of care and sadness
Dwells the little child.

Like a brooklet's merry murmur
In the gloomy wood;
Birdlike music lightly breaking
Through the solitude.

Like the gleam when clouds are riven
At the morning's birth;
Like a smile of God from heaven,
Dropped upon the earth.

The Captain's Daughter.

WE were crowded in the cabin,
　　Not a soul would dare to sleep;
It was midnight on the waters,
　　And a storm was on the deep.

'T is a fearful thing in winter
　　To be shattered by the blast,
And to hear the rattling trumpet
　　Thunder, "Cut away the mast!"

So we shuddered there in silence,
　　For the stoutest held his breath,
While the hungry sea was roaring,
　　And the breakers talked with Death.

As thus we sat in darkness,
　　Each one busy with his prayers,
"We are lost!" the captain shouted
　　As he staggered down the stairs.

But his little daughter whispered,
　　As she took his icy hand,
"Isn't God upon the ocean,
　　Just the same as on the land?"

Then we kissed the little maiden,
And we spoke in better cheer; .
And we anchored safe in harbor
When the morn was shining clear.

James T. Fields.

Baby's First Tooth.

OUR mouth is a rose-bud,
And in it a pearl
Lies smiling and snowy,
My own little girl!

O, pure pearl of promise,
It is thy first tooth —
How closely thou shuttest
The rose-bud, forsooth!

But let me peep in it,
The fair thing to view;
Nay! only a minute;
Dear baby! now do!

You wont? little miser!
To hide the gem so;
Some day you 'll be wiser,
And show them, I know!

How dear is the pleasure —
My fears for thee past —
To know the white treasure
Has budded at last!

Fair child, may each hour
A rose-blossom be,
And hide in its flower
Some jewel for thee!

Frances Sargent Osgood.

Born — A Daughter.

A DAUGHTER!
Well, what brought her?
Kitty asks, "How came she here?"
Half with joy and half with fear.
Kitty is our eldest child —
Eight years old, and rather wild —
Wild in manner, but in mind
Wishing all things well defined.

Kitty says, "How came she here?
Father, tell me — it's so queer.
Yesterday we had no sister,
Else I'm sure I should have kissed her
When I went to bed last night,
And this morning hailed her sight
With a strange and new delight;

For, indeed, it passes all
To have a sister not so tall
As my doll; and with blue eyes;
And—I do declare!—it cries!

" Last night I did not see her, father,
Or I'm sure I had much rather
Stayed at home as still as a mouse
Than played all day at grandma's house.
She is pretty and so tiny—
And what makes her face so shiny?
Will it always be like that?
Will she swell up plump and fat,
Like my little doll? or tall
Like my wax one? tell me all
About her, papa dear,
For I do so long to hear
Where she came from and who brought
    her,
Yours and mamma's brand-new daugh-
    ter."

But, though the childish explanation
Be food enough for child's vexation,
We older folks must better find
To feed the hunger of the mind;
To us, of larger issues preaching,
This link of life eternal, reaching

From earth to heaven, this new-born soul
Come fresh and fair from wherever roll
Its countless years through yonder heaven
Has deeper cause for thinking given.

    A daughter!
No matter what—she comes to bring
A blessing in her life's young spring.
" No matter, darling — she is here —
Our daughter, sister, baby dear!
Open your hearts, and let her enter;
Open them wide, for God hath sent her."
Ladies' Repository.

O THOU bright thing, fresh from the hand
    of God,
The motions of thy dancing limbs are swayed
By the unceasing music of thy being!
Nearer I seem to God when looking on thee.
'T is ages since he made his youngest star;
His hand was on thee as 't was yesterday,
Thou later revelation! Silver stream,
Breaking with laughter from the lake divine
Whence all things flow! O bright and sing-
    ing babe,
What wilt thou be hereafter?
Alexander Smith.

A Child to Its Mother.

CRADLE me on thy knee, mamma,
   And sing the holy strain
That soothed me last, as you fondly
      pressed
My glowing cheek to your soft white breast;
For I saw a scene when I slumbered last
   That I fain would see again.

And smile as you then did smile, mamma,
   And weep as you then did weep;
Then fix on me thy glistening eye, .
And gaze and gaze till the tear be dry;
Then rock me gently, and sing, and sigh,
   Till you lull me fast asleep.

For I dreamed a heavenly dream, mamma,
   While slumbering on thy knee—
And I lived in a land where forms divine
In kingdoms of glory forever shine;
And the world I'd give, if the world were
      mine,
   Again that land to see.

I fancied we roamed in a wood, mamma,
   And we rested us under a bough;
Then near me a butterfly flaunted in pride,
And I chased it away through the forest wide,
And the night came on, and I lost my guide,
   And I knew not what to do.

My heart grew sick with fear, mamma,
   And I loudly cried for thee;
But a white-robed maiden appeared in the
     air,
And she flung back her curls of golden
     hair,
And she kissed me softly ere I was aware,
   Saying, "Come, pretty babe, with me.'

My tears and fears she beguiled, mamma
   And led me far away;
We entered the door of the dark, dark
     tomb;
We passed through a long, long vault of
     gloom;
Then opened our eyes on a land of bloom,
   And a sky of endless day.

And heavenly forms were there, mamma,
   And lovely cherubs bright;
They smiled when they saw me, but I was
     amazed,
And wondering, around me I gazed and
     gazed;
And sweet songs I heard, and sunny beams
     blazed
   All glorious in the land of light.

But soon came a shining throng, mamma,
    Of white-winged babes to me;
Their eyes looked love, and their sweet lips
        smiled,
And they marveled to meet with an earth-
        born child,
And they gloried that I from the earth was
        exiled,
    Saying, "Here, love, blest shalt thou be."

Then I mixed with that heavenly throng,
    mamma,
    A cherub and seraphim fair;
And saw, as I roamed through the regions of
        bliss,
The spirits which came from the world of
        distress,
And there was the joy no tongue can
        express,
    For they knew no sorrow there.

Do you mind when Sister Jane, mamma,
    Lay dead, a short time agone?
How you gazed on the sad and lovely wreck,
With a full flood of woe you could not check,
And your heart was so sad you wished it
        would break,
    But it loved; and you aye sobbed on.

But O! had you been with me, mamma,
    In the realms unknown to care,
And seen what I saw, you ne'er had cried,
Though they buried pretty Jane in the grave
       when she died;
For shining with the blest, and adorned like
    a bride,
    Sweet Sister Jane was there.

Do you mind that sick old man, mamma,
    Who came so late to our door,
When the night was dark, and the tempest
    loud,
And his heart was weak, but his soul was
    proud,
And his ragged old mantle served for his
    shroud
    Ere the midnight watch was o'er?

And think what a weight of woe, mamma,
    Made heavy each long-drawn sigh,
As the good man sat in papa's old chair,
While the rain dropped from his thin gray
    hair,
And fast the big tear of speechless care,
    Ran down from his glazing eye.
And think what a heavenward look, mamma,
    Flashed through each trembling eye,

As he told how he went to the Baron's
    stronghold,
Saying, "O, let me in, for the night is so
    cold!"
But the rich man cried, "Go sleep in the
    wold,
    For we shield no beggars here."

Well, he was in glory too, mamma,
    As happy as the blest can be;
He needed no alms in the mansions of light,
For he sat with patriarchs, clothed in white,
And there was not a seraph had a crown
    more bright,
    Nor a costlier robe, than he.

Now sing, for I fain would sleep, mamma,
    And dream as I dreamed before;
For sound was my slumber, and sweet was
    my rest
While my spirit in the kingdom of life was
    a guest,
And a heart that has throbbed in the realms
    of the blest
    Can love this world no more.

The Baby's Thoughts.

WHAT'S the baby thinking of?
Can you guess? Can you guess?
From between the budding leaves,
Underneath the cottage eaves,
Came an answer, "Yes, yes,
yes!"

"In the meadow," chirped the swallow,
"I was flying all the day;
I saw baby in the clover,
Toddling, tumbling, rolling over,
In his merry play;
Hiding in each grassy hollow,
Out of nurse's way.

"'Midst the buttercups I saw him;
He was humming like a bee;
And the daisies seemed to draw him,
For he crowed to see
All their white and pinky faces,
Starring over the green places,
'Neath the poplar-tree.
And the butterfly that pleased him,
And the May-bloom, out of reach,
And the little breeze that teased him,
He is thinking now of each.

Search his eyes, and you shall see
    King-cups, meshed in golden mazes,
    And a thousand starry daisies,
And a sunbeam, flashing free,
    And a little shifting shadow,
    Such as fluttered o'er the meadow,
        From the fluttering tree.

" Kiss his lip, and taste the rare
    Honey-sweetness lingering on it ;
Kiss his pretty forehead fair,
    May-bloom odors dropped upon it ;
And the naughty breezes also
    Kiss his cheek, and you shall find it
In the rich and rosy glow
    And the freshness left behind it.
On all these doth baby ponder,
And they wile him forth to wander
Still, through fields of scented clover,
Toddling, tumbling, rolling over ;
    Hiding in each grassy hollow."
Thus, between the budding leaves,
Underneath the cottage eaves,
    Answer made our friend the swallow.
                            Thomas Westwood.

Avails It Aught?

VAILS it whether bare or shod
These feet the path of duty trod?
If from the bowers of ease they
        fled
To seek affliction's humble shed;
If grandeur's guilty pride they spurned,
And home to virtue's cot returned,—
These feet with angel's wings shall rise,
And tread the palace of the skies.

The Golden Ringlet.

ERE is a little golden tress
    Of soft, unbraided hair;
'Tis all that's left of loveliness
    That once was thought so fair;
And yet, though time hath dimmed its
        sheen,
    Though all beside hath fled,
I hold it here, a link between
    My spirit and the dead.

Yes; from this shining ringlet still
    A mournful memory springs,
That melts my heart, and sends a thrill
    Through all its trembling strings.

I think of her, the loved, the wept,
  Upon whose forehead fair,
For eighteen years, like sunshine, slept
  This golden curl of hair.

Amelia B. Welby.

Pet's Early Morning Call.

TWO little feet I hear,
    Pattering on the floor
        Softly ;
  Two little eyes there are,
  Peeping through the door
        Slyly ;
Birds are piping morning song —
Cautiously he moves along,
    Lest he wake me.

Two little hands I feel,
  Resting on the spread
      Slightly ;
  Two little steps he takes
  O'er me — on the bed —
      Lightly ;
In his snow-white night-gown —
Carefully he lays him down,
    Lest he wake me.

Two little lips are soon
Pressing my lips down
    Sweetly;
Two little arms are there,
Twisting my neck round
   . Gently;
Roguishly his eyes meet mine —
Laughingly he says 'tis time
    I should wake me.

Little Maud.

WHERE is our dainty, our darling,
   The daintiest darling of all?
O where is the voice on the stairway?
   O where is the voice in the hall?
The little short steps in the entry,
   The silvery voice in the hall,
O where is our dainty, our darling,
   The daintiest darling of all,
       Little Maud?

The peaches are ripe in the garden,
   The apricots ready to fall;
The blue grapes are dripping their honey
   In sunshine upon the white wall;

O where are the lips, full and melting,
   That looked up so pouting and red,
When we dangled the sun-purpled bunches
   Of Isabels over her head?
O Maud! little Maud! say, where are you?
   (She never replies to our call!)
O where is our dainty, our darling,
   The daintiest darling of all,
         Little Maud?

———•———

MYSTERY! Mystery!
   Holy and strange;
What a life-history,
   Fruitful of change,
   And endless of range,
Is folded here, sweet within sweet, like a
       blossom,
   Darling of Paradise,
   Pure as the dew,
   Dropping from the starry skies,
   With their rich hue
   In their eyes blue;
O, dearer than life is thy weight on my
       bosom!
           S. C. Merrigate.

Baby Looking Out for Me.

WO little busy hands, patting on
the window;
Two laughing bright eyes looking
out at me;
Two rosy-red cheeks dented with dimples;
Mother-bird is coming: baby, do you see?

Down by the lilac-bush, something white
and azure,
Saw I in the window as I passed the tree;
Well I knew the apron and shoulder-knots
of ribbon,
All belonged to baby looking out for me.

Talking low and tenderly
To myself, as mothers will,
Spake I softly: " God in heaven,
Keep my darling free from ill!
Worldly gear and worldly honors
Ask I not for her from thee;
But from want, and sin, and sorrow,
Keep her ever pure and free."

* * * * *

Two little waxen hands
Folded soft and silently;
Two little curtained eyes
Looking out no more for me.

Two little snowy cheeks
　Dimple-dented never more ;
Two little trodden shoes
　That will never touch the floor ;
Shoulder-ribbons softly twisted,
　Apron folded, clean and white ;
These are left me — and these only —
　Of the childish presence bright.

Thus He sent an answer to my earnest
　　praying,
　Thus he keeps my darling free from
　　earthly stain ;
Thus he folds the pet lamb safe from earth-
　ly straying,
　But I miss her sadly by the window-pane,
Till I look above it ; then, with purer vision,
　Sad, I weep no longer the lilac-bush to
　　pass,
For I see her, angel, pure and white and
　sinless,
　Walking with the harpers by the sea of
　　glass.

　　Two little snowy wings
　　　Softly flutter to and fro ;
　　Two tiny childish hands
　　　Beckon still to me below ;

Two tender angel eyes
   Watch me ever earnestly;
Through the loop-holes of the stars
   Baby's looking out for me.

Claribel's Prayers.

THE day, with cold, gray feet, clung
   shivering to the hills,
   While o'er the valley still night's
    rain-fringed curtains fell;
But waking Blue Eyes smiled, "'T is ever
   as God wills;
He knoweth best, and be it rain or shine,
   't is well,
Praise God!" cried always little Claribel.

Then sank she on her knees; with eager,
   lifted hands
   Her rosy lips made haste some dear re-
    quest to tell:
"O, Father, smile, and save this fairest of
   all lands,
   And make her *free*, whatever hearts
    rebel!
Amen! Praise God!" cried little Claribel.

" And, Father," still arose another pleading
    prayer,
  " O save my brother, in the rain of shot
    and shell!
Let not the death-bolt, with its horrid,
    streaming hair,
  Dash light from those sweet eyes I love so
    well.
  Amen! Praise God!" wept little Claribel.

" But, Father, grant that when the glorious
    fight is done,
  And up the crimson sky the shouts of
    freemen swell,
Grant that there be no nobler victor 'neath
    the sun
  Than he whose golden hair I love so well.
  Amen! Praise God!" cried little Claribel.

When gray and dreary day shook hands with
    grayer night,
  The heavy air was thrilled with clangor
    of a bell.
" O, shout!" the herald cried, his worn eyes
    brimmed with light;
  " 'T is victory! O, what glorious news to
    tell!"
  " Praise God! He heard my prayer!"
    cried Claribel.

"But pray you, soldier, was my brother in
    the fight
  And in the fiery rain? O! fought he
    brave and well?"
"Dear child," the herald cried, "there was
    no braver sight
  Than his young form, so grand 'mid shot
    and shell."
  "Praise God!" cried trembling little
    Claribel.

"And rides he now with victor's plumes of
    red,
  While trumpets' golden throats his coming
    steps foretell?"
The herald dropped a tear. "Dear child,"
    he softly said,
  "Thy brother evermore with *conquerors*
    shall dwell."
  "Praise God! He heard my prayer!"
    cried Claribel.

"With victors wearing *crowns,* and bearing
    palms," he said
  A snow of sudden fear upon the rose lips
    fell.
"O, sweetest herald, say my brother *lives!*"
    she plead.

13

"Dear child, he walks with angels, who
    in strength excel.
Praise God, who gave this glory, Claribel!"

The cold, gray day died sobbing on the
    weary hills,
While bitter mourning on the night wind
    rose and fell.
"O, child," the herald wept, "'t is as the
    dear Lord wills;
He knoweth best, and, be it life or death,
    't is *well.*"
"Amen! Praise God!" sobbed little
    Claribel.   ***Linda Palmer.***

Little Feet and Little Hands.

LITTLE feet and little hands,
    Busy all the day,
    Never staying, in your playing,
    Long upon your way;
Little knowing whither going,
    Come to me, I pray!
Bring the sweetness, in its fleetness,
    Of the early flowers;
All the blessings and caressings
    Of your sunny hours!

Little feet and little hands,
    What awaits for you?
Sad to-morrows, with their sorrows,
    Clouds, or skies of blue?
Will the pleasures come with treasures
    Ever glad and new?
Never tarry feet that carry
    Little ones along;
May they bear the darlings where
    The air is full of song!

Little feet and little hands,
    Ye are wondrous fair!
Ye are straying, in your playing,
    From a balmy air.
Gently blowing, never knowing
    Any thought of care,
To its breezes. If it pleases
    Him who guides our way,
May you wander over yonder
    Where they ever play,
And no smiling or beguiling
    Woo again to stray!

A THING of beauty is a joy forever;
Its loveliness increases; it will never
Pass into nothingness.

The Dark.

HERE do the chickens run
  When they are afraid?
Out of the light, out of the sun,
  Into the dark, into the shade,
Under their mother's downy wing,
No longer afraid of any thing.

Dear little girl, dear little boy,
  Afraid of the dark,
Bid you good-bye to the daylight with joy,
  Be glad of the night; for, hark,
The darkness no danger at all can bring;
It is the shadow of God's wing.

Where do the little violets creep
  In the time of snow?
Into the dark, to rest and sleep,
  And to wait for the spring, they go
Under the ground where no storm can reach,
And God takes tender care of each.

Are you afraid, little girl or boy,
  Of the dark of death?
Jesus will carry you, full of joy,
  To the world of light, he saith:
Under the ground, where the violets sleep,
Your little body the Lord will keep.

Little Children.

PORTING through the forest wide;
Playing by the waterside;
Wandering o'er the heather fells;
Down within the woodland dells;
All among the mountains wild,
Dwelleth many a little child.

In the baron's hall of pride;
By the poor man's dull fireside;
'Mid the mighty, 'mid the mean,
Little children may be seen,
Like the flowers that spring up fair,
Bright and countless, every-where.

In the far isles of the main;
In the desert's lone domain;
In the savage mountain-glen,
'Mong the tribes of swarthy men;
Wheresoe'er a foot hath gone;
Wheresoe'er the sun hath shone
On a league of peopled ground,
Little children may be found.

Blessings on them! they in me
Move a kindly sympathy,

With their wishes, hopes, and fears;
With their laughter and their tears;
With their wonder so intense,
And their small experience.

Little children, not alone
On the wide earth are ye known,
'Mid its labors and its cares,
'Mid its sufferings and its snares;
Free from sorrow, free from strife,
In the world of love and life,
Where no sinful thing hath trod —
In the presence of your God,
Spotless, blameless, glorified —
Little children, ye abide!

Mary Howitt.

Child's Dream of Heaven.

MOTHER, come to my bedside,
  For God in love has given
The brightest, happiest dream to me;
  It must have come from heaven.

I and some friends of mine
  Seemed walking out together
Along the green and flowery fields
  In glad, warm, summer weather;

Till to a garden bright we came,
  With silver gates so fair,
Which made sweet music as they turned
  To let me enter there.

And flowers of every form and hue
  Grew all that garden o'er;
But flowers so fair, so bright, so sweet,
  I never saw before.

And our poor Marian was there,
  Who died some weeks ago;
And many more, I've heard you say,
  Passed through great pain and woe.

But now no tears are in their eyes,
  No pain is on their brow;
You would not think they could have wept
  Were you to see them now.

With golden crowns upon their heads,
  And robes of dazzling white,
They smiled and bid us welcome there
  Into that garden bright;

And showed us golden crowns and robes
  Which we one day should wear;
But not quite yet, till we, like them,
  Had passed our trial here.

But, mother, all those lovely flowers,
  And skies which knew no gloom,
Did not make half the blessedness
  Of that sweet garden home;

Nor yet the robe of snowy white,
  The golden diadem;
Nor yet the band of blesséd friends
  Who welcome us to them.

But the Lord, who loved the little ones,
  Walked through that happy place;
I heard his voice; he spoke to me;
  Mother, I saw his face!

And I am, O, so happy now!
  Dear mother, weep not thus;
I know he has a crown for you,
  And you will come to us.

O, do not cry! I cannot grieve:
  For what are death and pain,
If we may only hear that voice
  And see that face again?

YET sometimes sudden sights of grace,
Such as the gladness of thy face,
O sinless babe, by God are given
To charm the wanderer back to heaven.

The American Boy.

"FATHER, look up and see that flag;
  How gracefully it flies;
Those pretty stripes, they seem to be
  A rainbow in the skies."
"It is your country's flag, my son,
  And proudly drinks the light;
O'er ocean's wave, in foreign climes,
  A symbol of our might."

"Father, what fearful noise is that,
  Like thundering in the clouds?
Why do the people wave their hats,
  And rush along in crowds?"
"It is the voice of cannonry —
  The glad shouts of the free;
This is a day to mem'ry dear;
  'Tis Freedom's Jubilee."

"I wish that I were now a man,
  I'd fire my cannon too;
And cheer as loudly as the rest;
  But, father, why don't you?"
"I'm getting old and weak, but still
  My heart is big with joy;
I've witnessed many a day like this;
  Shout you aloud, my boy."

"Hurrah, for Freedom's Jubilee!
God bless our native land!
And may I live to hold the sword
Of Freedom in my hand!"
"Well done, my boy! grow up and love
The land that gave you birth;
A land where freedom loves to dwell
Is paradise on earth."

J. H. Hewitt.

Baby Louise.

'M in love with you, Baby Louise!
With your silken hair and your soft
blue eyes,
And the dreamy wisdom that in them
lies;
And the faint, sweet smile you brought from
the skies —
God's sunshine, Baby Louise!

When you fold your hands, Baby Louise,
Your hands, like a fairy's so tiny and fair,
With a pretty, innocent, saint-like air,
Are you trying to think of some **angel**-
taught prayer
You learned above, Baby Louise?

I'm in love with you, Baby Louise!
Why, you never raise your beautiful head!
Some day, little one, your cheek will grow
    red
With a flush of delight to hear the words
    said,
  "I love you," Baby Louise.

Do you hear me, Baby Louise?
I have sung your praises for nearly an hour,
And your lashes keep drooping lower and
    lower,
And — you've gone to sleep, like a weary
    flower,
  Ungrateful Baby Louise!
                Margaret Eytinge.

Shall the Baby Stay?

N a little brown house,
  With scarce room for a mouse,
  Came, with morning's first ray,
  One remarkable day,
(Though who told her the way
I am sure I can't say,)
A young lady so wee
That you scarcely could see

Her small speck of a nose ;
And, to speak of her toes,
Though it seems hardly fair,
Since they scarcely were there,
Keep them covered we must ;
You must take them on trust.

Now this little brown house,
With scarce room for a mouse,
Was quite full of small boys,
With their books and their toys,
Their wild bustle and noise.

" My dear lads," quoth papa,
" We 've too many by far ;
Tell us what can we do,
With this damsel so blue ?
We 've no room for her here,
So to me 't is quite clear,
Though it gives me great pain,
I must leave her again
With her white blanket round her,
Just as Nurse Russell found her."

Said stout little Ned,
" I 'll stay all day in bed,
Squeezed up nice and small
Very close to the wall."

Then spoke Tommy: " I 'll go
To the cellar below;
I 'll just travel about,
But not try to get out
Till you 're all fast asleep,
Then up stairs I will creep;
And so quiet I 'll be
You 'll not dream it is me."

Then flaxen-haired Will:
" I 'll be dreffully still;
On the back-stairs I 'll stay,
Way off, out of way."

Master Johnny the fair
Shook his bright, curly hair:
" Here 's a nice place for me,
Dear papa, do you see?
I just fit in so tight
I could stand here all night."
And a niche in the wall
Held his figure, so small.

Quoth the father, " Well done,
My brave darlings, come on!
Here 's a shoulder for Will;
Pray sit still, sir, sit still!
Valiant Thomas, for thee,
A good seat on my knee.

And Edward, thy brother,
Can perch on the other.
Baby John, take my back;
Now, who says we can't pack?

"So Love gives us room
And our birdie shall stay;
We'll keep her, my boys,
Till God takes her away."

Christian Register.

𝕳𝖊 𝖂𝖆𝖓𝖙𝖘 𝕾𝖚𝖈𝖍 𝕭𝖚𝖉𝖘.

SAW a beautiful child at play
  Among the flowers,
When a strange old man came round
   that way
  In the early hours.

"I will shorten thy sport, my bonny boy,"
  The old man said;
And he took from his hand each blurting
   toy,
  And the child was dead.

The old man gazed with a grim, cold smile
  On the lifeless one,
And he said, "They will call me dark and
   vile,
  For the service done."

"But my Master hath need of these holy
    gems
  In his garden fair;
He grafts such buds on undying stems
  To blossom there."

And he breathed in the ear of the sleeping
    boy
  That Master's name,
And the child sprang up with an eye of joy
  And a heart of flame.

And he cast his moldering robe aside —
  His robe of clay —
And he spread his wings in the sunny tide
  And soared away.

A mother's eyes were with weeping blurred
  Beside his bier:
For the triumph hymn of her soaring bird
  She could not hear.

Julia Scott.

The Boys.

HERE come the boys! O dear,
  the noise!
The whole house feels the racket
Behold the knee of Harry's pants,
  And weep o'er Bertie's jacket!

But never mind, if eyes keep bright,
    And limbs grow straight and limber;
We 'd rather lose the tree's whole bark
    Than find unsound the timber!

Now hear the tops and marbles roll!
    The floors — O, woe betide them!
And I must watch the balusters,
    For I know boys who ride them!

Look well as you descend the stairs;
    I often find them haunted
By ghostly toys that make no noise
    Just when their noise is wanted.

The very chairs are tied in pairs,
    And made to prance and caper;
What swords are whittled out of sticks!
    What brave hats made of paper!

The dinner-bell peals loud and well,
    To tell the milkman 's coming;
And then the rush of "steam-car trains"
    Sets all our ears a-humming.

How oft I say, "What shall I do
    To keep these children quiet?"
If I could find a good receipt,
    I certainly should try it.

But what to do with these wild boys,
   And all their din and clatter,
Is really quite a grave affair —
   No laughing, trifling matter.

"Boys will be boys"— *but not for long;*
   Ah, could we bear about us
This thought—how very soon our boys
   Will learn to do without us —

How soon but tall and deep-voiced men
   Will gravely call us "Mother;"
Or we be stretching empty hands
   From this world to the other—

More gently we should chide the noise;
   And when night quells the racket,
Stitch in but loving thoughts and prayers
   While mending pants and jacket!
                S. M. W.

Found Dead in the Street.

THE labor is over and done;
   The sun has gone down in the
     west;
   The birds are asleep, every one,
And the world has gone to its rest—

Sleepers on beds of down,
   'Neath cover of silk and gold,
Soft as on roses new blown
   Slept the great monarch of old;

Sleepers on mother's breast,
   Sleepers happy and warm,
Cosy as birds in their nest,
   With never a thought of harm;

Sleepers in garrets high,
   'Neath coverlet ragged and old;
And one little sleeper all under the sky,
   Out in the night and cold!

Alone in the wide, wide world,
   Christless, motherless, he;
Begging or stealing to live, and whirled
   Like a waif on an angry sea.

The daisy looks up from the grass,
   Fresh from the fingers of night,
To welcome the birds as they pass,
   And drink in fresh rivers of light;

Sleepers on mother's breast
   Waken to summer and mirth;
But one little sleeper has gone to his rest,
   Never to waken on earth.

Dead — found dead in the street;
 All forsaken and lorn;
Damp from head to the feet
 With the dews of the sweet May morn.

Dead — for the want of a crust!
 Dead — in the cold night air!
Dead — and under the dust,
 Without ever a word of prayer;

In the heart of the wealthiest city
 In this most Christian land,
Without ever a word of pity,
 Or the touch of a kindly hand!

A Baby Song.

COME, white angels, to baby and me;
 Touch his blue eyes with the im-
  age of sleep,
  In his surprise he will cease to
   weep:
  Hush, child, the angels are coming
   to thee!

Come, white doves, to baby and me;
 Softly whirr in the silent air,
 Flutter about his golden hair:
Hark, child, the doves are cooing to thee!

Come, white lilies, to baby and me;
    Drowsily nod before his eyes,
    So full of wonder, so round, and wise:
Hist, child, the lily-bells tinkle for thee!

Come, white moon, to baby and me;
    Gently glide o'er the ocean of sleep,
    Silver the waves of its shadowy deep:
Sleep, child, the whitest of dreams to thee.

Heir of Immortality.

LIFE has just begun!
    Another soul has won
    The glorious spark of being.
    Pilgrim of life, all hail!
He who at first called forth
From nothingness the earth,
Who piled the mighty hills, and dug **the sea,**
    Who gave the stars to gem
    Night like a diadem,
    O blessed child! made thee.
Fair creature of the earth,
Heir of immortal life, though mortal in **thy**
       birth,
       Hail, all hail!

The Triad.

YOU have four, and I have three,
Jane, and Rose, and Emily.
Jane, my eldest, is sedate,
Fit to be a Crusoe's mate;
Quite a housewife in her way;
Busily employed all day.
When I 'm sleeping in my bed,
Jane is working overhead;
So correct, so kind, so sage,
She 's a wonder for her age.
And if I had half a score
Of the cleverest daughters more,
I should ne'er expect to gain
One so useful as my Jane!

Rose is quite a different child;
Tractable enough, and mild;
But the genius of the three,
The lady of the family;
With a voice so wondrous clear!
And for music such an ear!
All our friends are in amaze
At the skill with which she plays;
You may name whate'er you will,
Rose for any piece has skill!
Then she writes, and can succeed
In poems beautiful indeed.

She can design too, and I never
For a child saw aught so clever!
Heads she draws, and landscapes **too**,
Better far than I can do,
Though no little sum was spent
To give me that accomplishment.
She is quite an artist now —
Has it stamped upon her brow;
And I 'm sure will earn her bread
With that intellectual head!

Emily, my youngest elf,
Is the picture of myself;
For her age extremely tall,
And the idol of us all.
O, the little roguish thing!
Now she 'll dance, and now she 'll sing;
Now she 'll put on modish airs,
Such as Mrs. Johnson wears;
Shaking her rich, curling tresses,
For the plumes with which she dresses.
On my life, I sometimes fear
She will mimic her when here!

Emily is bold and wild,
Quite a beau-ideal child,
Spoiled enough to have her will,—
Loving yet, and gentle still;

Just as poets say should be
The youngest of the family;
A little, happy, rosy pet;
One of pretty names to get,
Puck, and Mab, and Mignonnette!

Mrs. Howitt.

--------•--------

Night Song.

MOTHER, now sing me to rest,
   For the long, long day is done;
Fold me to sleep on thy breast,
   As the night folds up the sun.

For my heart is heavy with fears,
   And my feet are weary with play;
Hide me from life's lengthened years —
   Fold me from weeping away.

These flowers, so blessed and sweet,
   I 've gathered from far and from near;
I lay them all down at thy feet —
   They are wet with many a tear.

But, mother, now sing me to rest;
   Take back the lone child, tired with
      playing;
Fold me to sleep on thy breast —
   All the day long vainly straying.

"Our Nellie."

A SWEET little face beaming sunni-
est gladness,
Unconsciously banishing weari-
some care;
A musical voice, touching no chords of sad-
ness;
There's joy in the household if Nellie is
near.

She conquers the heart with the bright in-
spiration
Of childhood's simplicity, innocence,
truth;
She lisps forth, "I love you!" without res-
ervation;
A warm place is open to Nellie henceforth.

Forgetfulness comes as she prattles, unwit-
ting,
That life has its cares as the years bear
us on;
A radiance is thrown over earth most befit-
ting,
And fairest of flowers in our pathway are
strewn.

Can grief be in store for thee, dear little
    sunbeam ?
So trusting and artless, can thy heart be
    chilled ?
Shall storms overtake, wrecking some cher-
    ished day dream ?
Thy cup overflowing, with anguish be
    filled ?

May Heaven avert such a destiny, darling!
    May He who the "little ones" guards
    shelter thee!
May Nellie be blithesome through all her
    life's morning!
    Its evening brightened by love ever be.
                    S.

The Moorland Child.

PON the bleak and barren moor
    I met a wandering child;
    Her cheeks were pale, her hair
        hung lank,
    Her sunken eyes gleamed wild.

"And have you no kind mother, child?"
    I asked, with softened tone.
"My mother went away lang syne,
    And left me here alone.

" 'T was in the winter weather; black
  The night lay on the moor;
The angry winds went howling by
  Our creaking cottage door;

" My mother lay upon her bed,
  She shook and shivered sore;
She clasped me in her trembling arms,
  She kissed me o'er and o'er.

"I knelt beside her on the ground,
  I wailed in bitter sorrow;
The wind without upon the moor
  My wailings seemed to borrow.

" My mother strove to soothe my grief;
  But while she spoke, alas!
Across her sunken face I saw
  A sudden shadow pass.

"And she fell back, so weak and wan,
  O, sir! I never heard
Her voice again, or caught the sound
  Of one fond farewell word!

" The bleak wind blew — my eyes were dry;
  I hushed my bitter moan;
But I knew that she was gone away,
  And I was left alone.

" The bleak wind blew — the heavy hail
  On hill and holt was driven;
But she went up the golden stair,
  And through the gate of heaven.

" They bore her to the church-yard grave;
  The little daisies love it;
But I never sit the mound beside,
  Nor shed a tear above it.

" My mother is not there; in dreams,
  When winter woods are hoary,
I see her on the golden stair,
  Beside the gate of glory.

" Her eyes are calm, her forehead shines,
  Amid the heavenly splendor;
On earth her face was kind, but ne'er
  Wore smiles so sweet and tender.

" And, sir, one night, not long ago, —
  December storms were beating, —
I heard her voice, so fond and clear,
  Float down, my name repeating.

" The fir-trees rocked upon the hill,
  And blast to blast was calling —
She said, 'The earth is dark and drear;
  Come home, come home, my darling.'

" The bleak wind blew — the heavy hail
  On hill and holt was driven ;
She said, ' Come up the golden stair,
  And through the gate of heaven ! '

" And soon, O soon"——But here her speech
  Broke off ; a sudden lightness
Passed o'er the child's pale cheek and brow,
  As with a sunbeam's brightness, —

And she went wandering o'er the moor,
  Low crooning some wild ditty ;
" God's calm," I said, " be on her shed,
  And God's exceeding pity ! "
                  Thomas Westwood.

Index.

CPSIA information can be obtained at www.ICGtesting.com
Printed in the USA
LVOW012104221111

256124LV00021B/187/P